INTERNET ADVENTURES
for Young Children
101 Websites and Hands-on Activities

by Catherine H. Cook
and Janet M. Pfeifer

Incentive Publications, Inc.
Nashville, Tennessee

With love to
Everett, Anderson, and Virginia
and
Philip, Peggy, and Olivia

Thank you for the inspiration.

Illustrated by Gayle S. Harvey
Cover by Geoffrey Brittingham
Edited by Jennifer E. Janke

Library of Congress Catalog Card Number: 99-71590
ISBN 0-86530-435-1

PRINTED IN THE UNITED STATES OF AMERICA

Guide to the Adventures

INTRODUCTION

When children explore the Internet, they can virtually walk the Great Wall of China, peruse shelves of distant libraries, tour museums the world over, or listen to the sounds of barnyard animals. It is an unequaled resource for information, education, and entertainment. Children need to become adept at using the Internet in order to compete in schools today and in the workplace tomorrow. However, the task of locating a decent website can be both difficult and time-consuming for many parents and educators. Moreover, children should not surf the Net independently, either using their computers like smart televisions or exploring sites that are inappropriate. Recognizing this dilemma, teachers and parents alike are seeking safe, fun, and easy ways to introduce young children to the technology of the 21st century. *Internet Adventures for Young Children* provides just such a resource.

This book directs parents and teachers of children ages 4–7 to high-quality, educational, and age-appropriate websites. Each page begins with a topic and includes a website name, address, and description, as well as a corresponding activity and materials list. The book explores everything of interest to young children, including animals, art and music, education, entertainment, fun and games, geography and travel, history, holidays, science, and sports. By coupling an appropriate website with a complementary activity, young children are provided with a way to use their computers and the Internet in a positive, hands-on, interactive manner. Through our book, kids build castles out of cardboard boxes, paint and decorate them, play in them, then log on and travel to Europe to explore real castles that are hundreds of years old.

While we guarantee that the sites in our book are child-friendly, we cannot guarantee that the links provided by each site are safe. Monitor your child's exploration of those links. In addition, the Internet is quickly changing and websites sometimes move around or disappear entirely. We have tried to include only those websites that would stand the test of time. Some of our sites are sponsored by educational, governmental, or non-profit organizations. Many of our sites are funded by corporations, moviemakers, and other for-profit groups. Our intention is to provide our readers with a broad spectrum of websites from which to choose. In an effort to ensure that readers will be able to access current websites on the internet, the authors have created a website readers can visit should they discover a web address referenced in this book is no longer valid. The address of this website is: http://members.aol.com/iaforkids/InternetAdventures/index.htm . Please also visit our website to submit suggestions for other sites and questions about current sites.

The first website in the book is on Internet Safety. Be sure to read and explore this topic thoroughly. The Internet is a wonderful new resource for communicating and gathering information, but one that must be used with caution. You can never be too safe.

All of our websites are accompanied by suggestions for activities. These activities are meant to encourage using the website as a springboard for other related learning experiences. Let your imagination and creative instincts guide you and the children. We hope you enjoy using the book as a positive way to introduce your young children to the wonders of the Internet.

"Remember, it's not the technology, but how it is used, that makes a difference."
(America Online Parents' Guide to Cyberspace, 9/9/98)

INTERNET TIPS AND TERMS

The World Wide Web, Internet, or **Cyberspace** refers to the electronic connection or link of computers around the world via cables and modems.

Modem is the device that transmits information for computers to and from the Internet. The higher the modem speed, the faster the transmission time. The modem connects to the World Wide Web (WWW) through a Web Browser and an Internet Service Provider (ISP).

Web Browser is the program your computer uses to retrieve, read, and process the information available on other websites. Your browser (the most widely used being Microsoft Explorer and Netscape Navigator) provides you with e-mail and other tools for making the Internet easier to use. The browser has the following features which make the Internet user-friendly:

> **Bookmark** stores a website's address in a folder for easy access.
>
> **Maximize** is used to enlarge a website's screen to make it easier to read.
>
> **Minimize** is used to reduce a website's screen in order to look at other programs or pages without leaving a website.
>
> **Forward** is used to flip forward through links and pages previously viewed during current Internet sessions.
>
> **Back** is used to back through links and pages that you have previously viewed during current Internet sessions.

Internet Service Provider is the company you use to provide you with access to the Internet. America Online (AOL) and CompuServe are some of the more widely used ISPs. The service may be a portal (providing channel routes to other sources on the web) or a service provider that provides only a connection to the Internet and leaves it to you to find your own information on the web.

Website and **web page** are the places on the Internet that you "visit." People, businesses, and government agencies create and post a web page, or a website made up of many pages, on the Internet. Typing in web addresses accesses the websites.

Web address is the address you type into your web browser to go to a specific page on the Internet. Most addresses are case sensitive—the address must be typed exactly as it appears in either upper case or lower case letters. Some websites do not allow for error when it comes to locating an address.

Links are websites easily accessed by clicking a keyword, title or phrase within another address. For example, a website about ants provides access or links to other sites related to the topic "ants." Instead of typing in the new website address, you can click on the pre-addressed title and let the browser take you there. A search engine can be used to find links to topics of interest on the web.

Search engines are programs on the Internet designed to locate websites that pertain to keywords or listed topics. For example, Metacrawler is the search engine we most often used when researching this book. We typed in a key word or topic at the Metacrawler website and the Metacrawler search engine "crawled" around the World Wide Web (in a matter of seconds) and located websites related to the topic. It then provided links and described those links in order of relevance to the topic. We followed the links to find appropriate websites. This site is efficient and comprehensive, but it is not a child-safe search engine.

Child-safe search engines are search engines designed to provide links to child-safe sites and weed out inappropriate websites. Adults need to be aware that website designers can manipulate names in their web pages so that search engines will retrieve their website. For example, http://www.whitehouse.gov takes you to the White House in the United States. However, http://www.whitehouse.com is a pornography site. Child-safe search engines will help prevent these unwanted links from appearing in your search results.

Delete Temporary Internet Files is a function used to delete files you are not using in order to speed up transmission time. Your computer will temporarily store the information gathered when on the Internet. Periodically delete your temporary Internet files to keep the computer from storing a huge surplus of information.

How to Conduct a Safe Internet Search

It is easy to find information on the Internet if you know where to look. Search engines are websites that scan the entire Internet for specific information in a matter of seconds. Log on to the search engine website and enter a key word. For instance, if you want to learn about George Washington, go to a search engine and type in the words "George Washington." A list of relevant websites will appear with a brief description of what can be found at each site. Depending on what your interests are, you can choose the site that best fits your needs. You may need to visit several search engines as well as the sites within those search engines to find the information you are seeking.

Three of the best general search engines are:

Metacrawler® http://www.metacrawler.com
Lycos® http://lycos.cs.cmu.edu/
Yahoo® http://www.yahoo.com/

To conduct the safest search possible, use one of the two best automated child-safe search engines:

AltaVista™ **Family Filter** http://jump.altavista.com/
Searchopolis℠ http://www.searchopolis.com

Happy hunting!

Safety on the Web

Website:

Safety on the Web

Address:

http://www.safekids.com

The Internet is a fun place for kids to explore, but just like the park down the street, or other great places you visit, there are certain rules you should follow to ensure a safe experience. The Safe Kids website educates adults and children about possible problems lurking in cyberspace by presenting the risks of randomly surfing the net, as well as providing specific guidelines for adults on how to reduce these risks. Read *My Rules for Cyber Space*, and print out the six basic rules of Internet safety. The site offers a **Directory of Parental Control Software**, links to articles on Internet safety, and links to safe search engines for children. Bookmark the **Child-Safe Search Engines** as a favorite place in your web browser. Children ages 4–7 should not be allowed to search alone, and when surfing with children, adults should use only search engines that are child-safe. Remember, when researching topics using popular (but not kid-safe) search engines, links to offensive websites are not filtered from the user.

Activity:

Discuss the Internet rules of safety with your children. Together formulate and write down rules for the information superhighway. Post them near the computer where they can be seen at all times. Practice the safety guidelines with your children by presenting them with hypothetical situations. Explore solutions together, so that your kids will know what to do if they find themselves in a questionable situation. Now would be a great time to go over other important safety rules: Don't talk to strangers. Buckle up. Wear a helmet. Stop, drop, and roll. Design a classroom or family fire escape plan, and designate a meeting place in case of fire. Always, always, say NO to drugs! Have kids learn their address and phone number.

Materials:

Pen   Paper

Animals live everywhere—on the African plains, in the deep dark jungle, and even in your own backyard or playground. In order to see a specific animal, you have to know where in the world to look. To find your animal friends on the web, you have to have a website address. There are thousands of web pages available on line, and the number grows every day. Each web page contains its own specific information and can only be found at a specific web address or URL (Uniform Resource Locator). A URL can be case-sensitive, so be sure to type it exactly as it appears, using either upper or lower case letters. The characters and letters within the address can sometimes tell you something about the organization sponsoring the website. Examples are:

.com—commercial   .mil—military

.org—non-profit organization   .ca—originates in Canada

.gov—government agency   .jp—originates in Japan

.edu—educational institution

So, remember to get the web address right—and enjoy your trip through the animal kingdom!

Animals

Ants

Website:

Gakken's Photo Encyclopedia "Ants"

Address:

http://www.dna.affrc.go.jp/htdocs/

Ant.WWW/INTRODUCTION/Gakken79E/title.html

Ants are everywhere—sometimes marching in a line across the kitchen floor, in search of a forgotten cookie crumb, in the yard building an anthill, or at the park swarming around Kool-Aid spills. Children are fascinated with and naturally curious about ants, since ants are one of the few beings in their world that are actually smaller than they are. This site explores in detail the life of the ant and its community. Come and learn about the hundreds of species of ants—there are 262 different species living in Japan alone. Find out what enemies ants have, learn about the strength of the ant body, and discover what ants do in the winter. View pictures of ants and their curious behavior. There are interesting instructions on how to catch, keep, care for, and conduct research on ants.

> **Bonus site:** 3D insects Department of Entomology Virginia Tech
>
> http://www.ento.vt.edu/~sharov/3d/3dinsect.html
>
> Build, view, and interact with your own virtual 3-D insects.

Activity:

Make a bug house out of an empty jar. Clean an empty jar (jelly, peanut butter, or mayonnaise) and poke air holes in the lid. Fill ⅓ of the jar with dirt; sprinkle in small twigs, dried leaves, and small seeds. Collect some bugs for observation and secure the lid of the jar. You can collect ants and watch them build tunnels in the dirt. If you collect ants, place the jar in a water bath (a pie plate filled with water). This will prevent the ants from escaping from the jar. Observe your bugs for only a day, then release them where you found them. Study different bugs and their habits, discuss the different bugs that you catch, and compare their similarities and their differences.

Materials:

Clean jar with lid   Dried leaves, twigs, and seeds
Dirt   Bugs

Dinosaur Mania

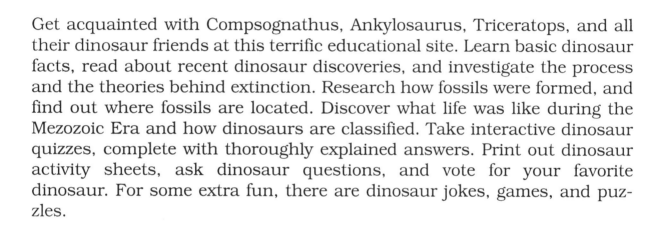

Website:

Zoom Dinosaurs.com

Address:

http://www.zoomdinosaurs.com/subjects/dinosaurs/toc.shtml

Get acquainted with Compsognathus, Ankylosaurus, Triceratops, and all their dinosaur friends at this terrific educational site. Learn basic dinosaur facts, read about recent dinosaur discoveries, and investigate the process and the theories behind extinction. Research how fossils were formed, and find out where fossils are located. Discover what life was like during the Mezozoic Era and how dinosaurs are classified. Take interactive dinosaur quizzes, complete with thoroughly explained answers. Print out dinosaur activity sheets, ask dinosaur questions, and vote for your favorite dinosaur. For some extra fun, there are dinosaur jokes, games, and puzzles.

Activity:

Make dinosaur eggs. Hardboil eggs and dye them in a mixture of vinegar and food coloring, following the egg-dyeing instructions on most boxes of food coloring. While they are drying, use a hole punch to make circles out of multicolored paper. After the eggs are dry, apply the circles to eggs with glue, then coat the entire shell with clear spray-on varnish. The eggs should last as decorations for about two weeks at room temperature, but be sure not to eat them!

Materials:

Eggs
Vinegar
Food coloring
Hole punch
Colored paper
Glue
Spray-on clear varnish

Farm Animals

Website:

Kid's Farm

Address:

http://www.kidsfarm.com/

Little farm hands can strut and square dance to the great "down-home" music playing at this site. Spend a day with domestic and wild animals, and meet the people on a working ranch in Colorado. Ride in the **Kiddie Rodeo,** and check out what's new at the ranch. View pictures, listen to the chirping of 42 new baby chicks, and watch as the rehabilitation center nurses a 4 week old baby raccoon and returns him to the wild. Meet all kinds of working animals at the **Farm Animals** page. Children love Jack and Jill, the Belgian draft horses, with their beautiful manes, and tails longer than 5 feet! Visit with the brave dogs that keep watch over all the other animals on the ranch, and see the German Shepherd guide three lost sheep back to the ranch. Listen to the baby sheep and their mother as the lost sheep find their way back to the herd. Meet Willow and Goofy, the baby beavers, who were saved by the rehabilitation center. Some of the pets in the rehab center were named from kids' suggestions over the Internet. Submit your own ideas and keep checking back to see if your suggestion is given to one of the farm animals.

Activity:

Make stamp art with potato prints. Pick a few potatoes out of the garden or from the grocery store and get ready to paint. Adults: clean the potato, cut it in half, then draw and carve a design into the flat, cut part of the potato. Try carving farm designs to use as prints. Carve a barn, a cow with spots, horses, and a fence. Kids can then dip their stamps into tempera paint, blot on newspaper to remove excess paint, and press onto paper.

Materials:

Potatoes	Paint
Paper	Carving utensil

Leapin' Frogs

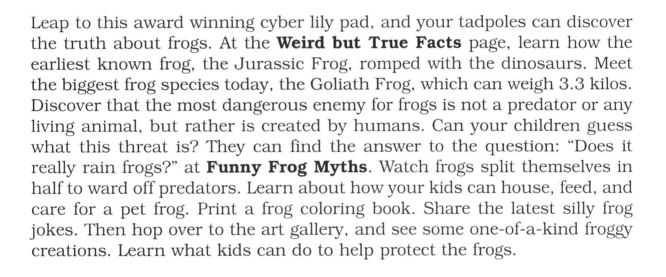

Website:

Frogland

Address: *AllAboutFrogs.org*

http://teleport.com/~dstroy/index.html

Leap to this award winning cyber lily pad, and your tadpoles can discover the truth about frogs. At the **Weird but True Facts** page, learn how the earliest known frog, the Jurassic Frog, romped with the dinosaurs. Meet the biggest frog species today, the Goliath Frog, which can weigh 3.3 kilos. Discover that the most dangerous enemy for frogs is not a predator or any living animal, but rather is created by humans. Can your children guess what this threat is? They can find the answer to the question: "Does it really rain frogs?" at **Funny Frog Myths**. Watch frogs split themselves in half to ward off predators. Learn about how your kids can house, feed, and care for a pet frog. Print a frog coloring book. Share the latest silly frog jokes. Then hop over to the art gallery, and see some one-of-a-kind froggy creations. Learn what kids can do to help protect the frogs.

Activity:

Frogs jump all day long. Spend a day hopping around like a frog! Try a game of leapfrog. One person squats low to the ground. Another person jumps over the person from behind while bracing their hands on the stooped person's back. Then the person who jumped squats down, and the sequence is repeated. Try a standing long jump. How far can you jump? How high can you jump? Try a running long jump. Do you jump farther running or standing? Do frogs jump farther running or standing? (Hint: frogs can't run!)

Milk A Cow

Website:

On the Moove

Address: DainyBiz.com

http://www.moomilk.com

"Drink your milk! It's good for you!" Sound familiar? Mooooove on over and learn how milk gets from the cow to the kitchen table. Take a virtual tour of a dairy farm at the **Story of Milk** page. Did you know that cows drink 30–40 gallons of water a day, and that some cows produce 19,000 pounds of milk a year? Learn the difference between Jersey (reddish brown) and Holstein (brown and black) cows. Did you know that a cow's black spots are like our fingerprints—no two are the same? Take a ride in special refrigerated trucks that pick up milk from the dairy farm and keep the milk cool, while it is transferred to the processing plant. Watch milk being pasteurized—boiled at 145 degrees. Learn the difference between whole and skim milk at the **I Want to Know** page. Play *Connect the Dots* with the cows to complete an entire dairy farm scene.

Activity:

Your budding dairy farmers can gain hands-on experience milking their own cows! Well, not exactly a cow, but the next best thing to a real udder. Fill a thin plastic surgical glove with water and secure the open end by tying it in a knot. Hang the plastic glove with fingers pointing down at waist height by tying it to the back of a chair. Place an empty bucket under the udder glove and poke tiny holes in the ends of the gloves with a small straight pin. Show your kids how to extract the milk by squeezing in a top to bottom motion.

Materials:

Thin surgical gloves
Straight pin
Pail

Sea Animals

Website:

Sea World/Busch Gardens®
Animal Information Database

Address:

http://www.seaworld.org/homepage.html

Come dance with the dolphins at Sea World! View the birth of the latest family member at Sea World in Orlando, Florida, and read about the amazing rescues of endangered animals. Watch **Shamu TV** to view film excerpts of sharks and killer whales. Set out on an **Aquatic Safari** and get acquainted with the creatures living on the ocean floor. **Animal Bytes** teaches kids facts about all kinds of animals. Have an animal question? **Ask Shamu** has the answers. Sail over to the **Shark Cam** and view pictures of live sharks as they swim and feed. In the **Sea World Songbook** you can learn the lyrics to animal tunes, such as "Scurry, Scurry, Little Crab."

Activity:

Create your own ocean. Fill a small jelly-size jar or soda bottle with a half cup of sand and small seashells, driftwood, or other bits of nature. Fill the jar halfway with mineral oil, add a drop of food coloring, and finish filling with rubbing alcohol. Close the lid and secure with masking tape. Make some waves by turning the jar from side to side.

Materials:

Blue food coloring
Jar or bottle with a lid
Mineral oil
Rubbing alcohol
Sea shells
Masking tape
Sand
Tape

The Zoo for You

Website:

The National Zoo Home Page

Address:

http://www.si.edu/natzoo

Welcome to the nation's first BioPark! Take an audio tour of the park and visit cheetahs, giant pandas, giraffes, and great apes. View animal photos, solve crossword puzzles and complete word searches, play the *Orangutan Language Project* game, and track elephants on their journeys. Watch videos like Amazonia, Golden Lion Tamarins, or Poison Arrow Frogs. You can plan a visit to the zoo (down to the very last detail), find out about the latest zoo births, and read about the Komodo dragon, a small lizard that has become an endangered species. If you can't actually get to the National Zoo, this is the next best thing.

Activity:

Make a zoo with your child's collection of stuffed animals. Separate the animals into groups based on species or habitat, then talk about what the animals eat, where they get their food, the region in which they live, and who their natural enemies are. Discuss what makes a good zoo and what makes a bad zoo. Encourage children to talk about why zoos are important and what we can learn from them. Research your child's favorite animal on the Internet or with an encyclopedia.

Materials:

Stuffed animals

Tiger Trail

Website:
The Tiger Information Center

Address:
http://www.5tigers.org

Three species of tigers have become extinct in the past 70 years, and only 6,000 tigers are left alive in the wild. Pounce on the **Tiger Information Center** to learn the plight of the world's tiger population and what you can do to help. View pictures of different types of tigers, then listen to tiger talk (growls, moans, and threats) at the **Multimedia** page. Prowl the **Cubs n' Kids** page to learn all about tigers. Do your children know that every tiger has a different pattern of stripes? Go to **Tiger Adventures** and help track tiger poachers (the tiger's biggest threat). Chase poachers across India, and help track an escaped tiger that is loose in a city. Plan a habitat for the tiger at the zoo. Learn what other kids from around the world are doing to help save the tigers.

Activity:

Fingerprint the whole class or family! Like a tiger's stripes, no two human fingerprints are alike. This is Mother Nature's way of telling us that we are special. Firmly press each person's index finger into a stamp pad, and press onto a piece of paper. If you don't have a stamp pad, cover a one-inch square heavily with pencil, and rub the finger in it, covering the fingertip well. Place a one-inch by two-inch-wide piece of clear tape on a flat surface, sticky side up. Place the finger firmly on the sticky side. Try not to smear it. Lift the finger straight off. Place the tape sticky side down onto a blank index card. Presto! You now have a one-of-a-kind fingerprint. Write the names of family members at the top of the card. Look at the different prints with a magnifying glass and observe the differences.

Materials:

Stamp pad	Index card
Tape	Pencil
Magnifying glass (optional)	

The World Wide Web allows you not only to read text, but also to experience the wonders of multimedia through your computer. This is what makes the art and music sites so much fun. In order to enjoy multimedia effects, you will need to download plug-ins, most of which are free. The most popular of these are Macromedia's Shockwave, Midi, and Network's Real-Audio. Websites will inform you when you need these plug-ins, and will often allow you to download from the site itself. Downloading is easy and often takes only a few minutes. It is worth the wait!

Art and Music

Art for Young Children

Website:

KinderArt™

Address:

http://www.kinderart.com/about.htm

Drawing, painting, printing, sculpture, and other lesson plans are available at this creative site that spans all age groups. A young child can opt for crayons and coloring pages, while the older artist can learn to experiment with pastels, watercolors, and, if you are feeling brave, ink. Once children have designed their original artwork, you can post it on the site's **Refrigerator Gallery** for all cyberspace to enjoy. Be sure to check out **Multicultural Art** for ideas from other parts of the world. **Art Across the Board** presents ways to incorporate art into science, math, and literature, and **Seasonal Themes** has ideas for different times of the year. There is also an extensive section of reference material, including specific activities for preschoolers, art terms, and articles and hints from the pros.

Activity:

Make a personalized name plate for each child's bedroom or desk with posterboard and tissue paper. Outline each child's name with a pencil in large letters on a piece of posterboard. Smear glue along the outline of the letters, one letter at a time, so that the glue does not dry too quickly. Tear up different colors of tissue paper into small pieces and apply to the gluey outline of the letter. Repeat with all the letters in the name and let dry. Try multicolored tissue paper or concentrate on one or two colors to match the décor of the child's bedroom or favorite colors.

Materials:

Posterboard
Tissue paper
Glue
Pencil

Build An Online Snowman

Website:

South Florida Snow Man

Address:

http://www.sun-sentinel.com/graphics/entertainment/snowman.htm

Children can build a snowman any day of the year at this creative and interactive site. Once the image of the snowman appears, each child can personalize her snowman in a variety of hats, clothes, and arms. Then, she can bring it to life with different kinds of eyes, noses and mouths. Experiment with different combinations as many times as you wish. For more fun, download a holiday coloring book, or take a test drive on Santa's sleigh. This is a fun winter site that children (and adults) of all ages can enjoy, without getting cold!

Activity:

Build a snowman out of cotton balls. Outline three circles with a pencil on a piece of cardboard, making the circles increase in size from top to bottom to make the head, torso, and base. Glue cotton balls inside the three circles. Add twig arms, and decorate with sequins, buttons, glitter, and fabric scraps. Let the snowman dry. Sing "Frosty the Snowman," and have an ice cream cone snack. This is a great activity for July when everyone needs to cool off!

Materials:

Cotton balls	Cardboard
Glue	Sequins and buttons
Fabric scraps	Glitter
Twigs	

Create with Crayons

Website:

Crayola®

Address:

http://www.crayola.com/

Take a tour of the Crayola assembly line and find out how crayons are made. Preschoolers can leap ahead and learn letters and numbers in the **Rainbow Room**. Big kids can visit the **Artists' Corner** for inspiration from some celebrated painters like Leonardo Da Vinci. Kids of all ages can scribble on over to the **Fun Facts** page to play *Crayon Trivia* and to learn how many crayons it would take to reach the moon. At this wonderful site, there are games to play, stories to read, pictures to color, and crafts to make.

Activity:

Finally, a use for all of those broken crayons! Create an original work of art by melting crayon shavings for a kaleidoscopic effect. Have the children pick out the crayon colors they want in their masterpiece, and shave the crayons using a hand held kitchen grater. (The grater should clean up easily with soap and water). Place one piece of wax paper on the table as a place mat. Sprinkle the colors in any design. Cover with a second piece of wax paper and remove to the ironing board. Iron the wax paper and watch the colors melt together. (Adults have to do the ironing, but kids can master the rest of the project.)

Materials:

> Wax paper
> Crayons
> Household iron
> Hand held grater

Cyber Etch–A–Sketch™

Website:

Etch-A-Sketch.com

Address:

http://etch-a-sketch.com/html/main.htm

What a toy! The terrific, timeless Etch-A-Sketch comes to you via the Internet. Use the online version of the real toy to make pictures. Join Etchy in his interactive stories, search for hidden numbers, letters, and shapes, and download coloring pages for offline art. Watch as each child's name is drawn in Etch-A-Sketch font. Find out where the aluminum powder for the Etch-A-Sketch comes from, and try to correctly answer trivia questions like "Who invented Etch-A-Sketch?" and "How many people work on the Etch-A-Sketch assembly line?" Be sure to check out **Tips and Tricks** for making your next Etch-A-Sketch creation your very best ever.

Activity:

Play a manual version of Etch-A-Sketch with your children. Begin by taking a pencil and drawing a line. Give the pencil to each child, and ask her to make the next line. Take turns adding one line at a time to the drawing until each child feels the drawing is complete. Ask the children to describe what they see on the page, then ask them to give the drawing a title. This is a wonderful, simple game encouraging imaginative thinking and creativity. Parents, this is also a great waiting room and car game to play with your child!

Materials:

Pencil and paper

Groovy School Music

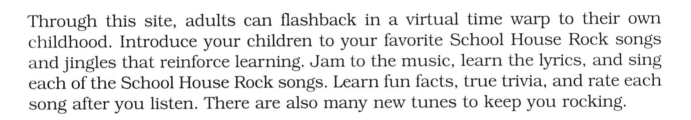

Website:

School House Rock!SM

Address:

http://genxtvland.simplenet.com/SchoolHouseRock/index-hi.shtml

Through this site, adults can flashback in a virtual time warp to their own childhood. Introduce your children to your favorite School House Rock songs and jingles that reinforce learning. Jam to the music, learn the lyrics, and sing each of the School House Rock songs. Learn fun facts, true trivia, and rate each song after you listen. There are also many new tunes to keep you rocking.

Bonus site: School House Rock lyrics

http://www.yak.net/pub/ian/SHR/Intro.html

The lyrics for all of the School House Rock songs are listed at this site.

Activity:

A time warp would not be complete without making a tie-dye T-shirt. Begin with a damp 100% cotton T-shirt. Lay it flat. Pick up 3 inches of the center of the T-shirt and twist, binding it with a rubber band. Repeat, twisting 3-inch sections until the entire T- shirt is bound. Put on plastic gloves. Mix water with dye (follow manufacturer's directions) and place in empty squeeze bottles. Mix the dye-activating solution. Soak T-shirt in dye-activator, then remove T-shirt to a large pan or tray. Color the bound sections of the T-shirt with dye, alternating color combinations. Saturate each section. Seal the shirt in a plastic bag for 24 hours. Rinse shirt, undo bands, and wash the shirt on gentle cycle.

Materials:

3 colors of cold water dye with manufacturer's recommended ingredients

100% cotton T-shirt

Rubber bands

Squeeze bottles

Large drip pan

Plastic gloves

Plastic bag

Music with Mozart

Website:

Mozart

Address:

http://www.stringsinthemountains.org/m2m/1once.htm

This is a super site for getting kids interested in classical music! Here, boys and girls can explore the life of a great musical genius, Johannes Chrysostomus Wolfgangus Theophillus Amadeus Mozart. (What a name! No wonder his family called him "Wolfie.") Read about how Mozart began to play the piano at age 3 and could play the violin as soon as he was given one at age 5. Read about and listen to Mozart's first minuet (piano solo). Find out who locked Mozart in a castle tower with only a paper and pen to determine if he was really writing the beautiful music. Travel Europe with Mozart as he plays for emperors, kings, and queens, and learn why royal interest in Mozart's music began to fade as he got older.

Activity:

Design a musical board game to teach your kids to distinguish musical sounds and instruments. Draw or cut out pictures from magazines of different instruments—piano, cymbals, drum, violin, trumpet, flute, harp, guitar, and include a picture of someone singing. Glue the pictures in rows on a 9 x 11 piece of posterboard. Listen to music together, and help the children recognize the different sounds by pointing out the instruments when you hear them. Parents can bring the board in the car when traveling and listen to tapes. When your child hears an instrument, she can cover the instrument's picture with a sticky note until all pictures in one row are covered. This game helps children appreciate music, as well as keeping them occupied during long car trips.

Materials:

Posterboard   Pictures of musical instruments
Glue   Self-stick notes

Musical Fun at Hop Pop Town

Website:

Hop Pop Town©

Address:

http://www.kids-space.org/HPT/index.html

Hop Pop Town© is designed to "encourage young children to improvise musical sequences, one of the vital factors necessary for young children to enjoy music." Rabbit and Raccoon will help your kids meet this goal at three different areas in Hop Pop Town—**Hoppy Hill, Poppy Street,** and **Hop Pop Hall.** The children can make animals play different sounds, hear scale tones by clicking on singing leaves, and figure out how instruments are divided into brass, strings, woodwinds, and other groups. They can also write a story at Hoppy Hill, play a brainteaser game, and listen to applause after they sing a song. This site is a nice introduction to music.

Activity:

Make your own band with instruments created in the kitchen. Hand out plastic bowls, sturdy wooden spoons, an eggbeater, and a small jar filled with dry beans. Encourage your children to take turns playing one at a time, then playing as a group. Record their music either on a tape recorder or video camera and play it back to them. Music can be created many different ways—ask your kids to come up with some others.

Materials:

      Kitchen objects and utensils
      Dried beans
      Tape recorder and audiotape or video camera (optional)

Musical Menagerie

Website:

Wonderland Home

Address:

http://wonderland.station.sony.com/wonderland/

There are more than 15 interactive games to choose from at the **Wonderland Station's Sandbox**. The **Sing-a-long Songbox** is a virtual boom box where kids can follow along with the words of their favorite songs. If your child likes books on tape, he or she will love **Webtime Stories'** *Hercules*, *Noah's Ark*, *Snow White* and *Treasure Island*. The computer reads the story as a child flips through the virtual pages of these on-line books. A junior playground is also available for the younger kids (ages 2–4).

Activity:

Experiment with musical tones by blowing into bottles. Collect 7 empty 10–16 ounce bottles. Leave one bottle empty and fill the rest of the bottles with different amounts of water, beginning with 1 inch of water, then increase an inch with each bottle, until the last bottle is almost full. Blow into different bottles to hear seven distinct and varied tunes. Are the tunes higher in pitch with more or less water? Try playing the tunes of your favorite songs with your bottles.

Materials:

7 empty 10–16 ounce bottles

Pencil Playground

Website:

Pencils! Pencils! Pencils!

Address:

http://www.pencils.com/

What would the world be like today if it were not for the invention of the pencil? Would education have spread to the masses without this easily created, transported, and distributed instrument of communication? Learn the history of the pencil, how it evolved from a stick of lead, to string-wrapped graphite, and finally, into the No. 2 pencil that we all know today. Learn why billions of pencils used in North America every year have erasers, while most of the pencils sold in Europe do not. Who makes these erasers, and what are they made of? Discover why 75% of pencils are yellow. Observe the difference between recyclable pencils, and learn how to avoid buying pencils made from rain forest woods. Don't forget to try the **Pencil Scavenger Hunt**.

Activity:

Personalize a pencil can or a box for storing all of your children's pencils and crayons. Choose from an empty soup can, frozen juice can, shoebox, or cigar box. Cover the rim of the empty container with tape. Paint or cover the box or can with felt or construction paper and decorate with glitter, markers, glue-on beads, or cut-up pictures from magazines. On a large label, have the child make a name plate and paste it onto the pencil holder.

Materials:

Empty soup can or small box	Felt or construction paper
Glue	Decorations
Large name label	Tape
Glitter	

Picture This

Website:

The Amazing Picture Machine

Address:

http://www.ncrtec.org/picture.htm

Questions, questions, questions! Kids are always asking questions. At this site you can find a picture of almost anything your child may ask you about. Enter a subject name and click. Within seconds, a picture will appear. The picture database is extensive, including pictures of musicians, 19th century writers, famous African-Americans, gems and minerals, and many other things. So the next time you are asked, "What do Manilas look like?" or "What does lichen look like?" you will be prepared to answer in a matter of seconds.

Activity:

Dabble in the art of photography by letting children take some of their own pictures. If you don't want to lend them your camera, there are several brands of plastic 110-millimeter film cameras that cost less than $20.00. You can also let them use a disposable 35-millimeter camera. Go on an outing and have the children photograph whatever interests them. If you are able, go together to get the film developed. If you go to a 1-hour photo lab, you might be able to watch the operators process the film. Let the children start a photo album. Assign each child one page to fill with her own pictures. If you consider this a year-long project, you will be able to see their photography skills improve. This is a great way to introduce children to the exciting art of photography.

Materials:

    Camera
    Film
    Photo album

Sand Sculptures

Website:
Gallery

Address:
http://www.sandsculpture.com/usagallery.htm

Playing in the sand will never be the same after a visit to this site. Before your next beach trip or summer vacation break, spend some time digging up award-winning ideas for sandcastles. The on-line art gallery at **Sand Sculptures of America** features contest winners and commercial designs from around the world. It is amazing that art of this caliber can be created out of such delicate material. There are amazing castles, wild animals (including gorillas, leopards, and tigers), snowmen, and many more wonders made out of sand. The sea life creations are so real that you feel as if the fish have escaped from the sea. Don't be alarmed by the dinosaurs—they are also made out of sand.

Activity:
Build a permanent sandcastle by sand casting with plaster of paris (found in craft stores). Mix up a batch of plaster of paris (follow manufacturer's instructions), and head for the sandbox with shovels and pails. Try making a castle by digging an 8-inch hole in the sand and sprinkling in stones and plastic gems. Or let your kids decide what they want to cast in the sand. Then pour in the plaster. You can also cast your child's footprints in the sand by pouring plaster into their bare footprints in the sand. Bring along some buckets of water, and try to make sculptures in the sand.

Materials:
Plaster of paris
Sand box
Shovels
Buckets
Sculpting tools

Internet Adventures

Sing your Favorite Songs at Kiddiddles

Website:

Kididdles

Address:

http://www.kididdles.com/

You want to teach your child a favorite song from your childhood, but the lyrics to "Oh Playmate, Come Out and Play with Me" are long forgotten. No problem! Find the words to lots of your favorite children's songs with MoJo, a singing and dancing mouse. The **Musical Mouseum** has songs organized alphabetically, and by category, for easier searching. Kids can also help add to a never-ending story by visiting Kiplink the elephant and his trunk full of tall tales. Then play *Rolette's Revenge,* and see if you can solve the puzzles that Loopity Lee has to offer. Visit **Sir Pinkster's Kididdles Kids** for a look at original artwork, funny jokes, and new songs, then add your own.

Activity:

Record the children singing their favorite songs. Make a copy to send home or give to relatives, and be sure to date the tape. Play the tape back for your children, and teach them where the rewind button is. They may want to listen to their songs over and over.

Materials:

Tape recorder
Audiotape

Learning new languages should be part of everyone's education. Computers even have their own language for communicating over the Internet—hypertext markup language, or HTML. When a Web page is designed, HTML is used to arrange the text and bring you the information in a format that is easy to read, use, and understand. HTML allows multimedia and text documents to be shared and enjoyed over the Internet. HTML has changed a lot in the past few years and will continue to evolve as the Internet moves at faster speeds. There is a new language being developed (Virtual Reality Modeling Language, or VRML), which makes it possible to create and explore 3-Dimensional applications over the Internet. Check out 3D Insects at http://www.ento.vt.edu/~sharov/3d/3dinsect.html to sample applications using VRML.

Education

Arithmetic

Website:

A+ Math

Address:

http://www.aplusmath.com/

Addition, subtraction, multiplication, division, and geometry can all be found at this cyber math lab. There are math games for all ages and levels of ability. Kids can practice manipulating numbers with virtual flash cards, or play interactive math games like *Matho*, a math bingo game, or *Math Concentration*, a game for solving tricky problems. Kids can play against the clock, and the winners are posted each day. Help with math homework can be found at **Homework Helper**. Enter a math problem with a proposed answer, and the Helper will verify the answer when it is correct. This site is maintained by two engineers and a teacher in an effort to promote math proficiency worldwide.

Activity:

Every trip to the grocery store can be a math lesson for young children. The youngest children delight in recognizing the numbers in prices of items. Older children can read the price and tell how much more or less it is than the nearest dollar amount. Let the children help you make out a grocery list. Estimate how much individual items are going to cost, then let them tell you how much the items really cost when you get to the store. Compare the actual cost to their estimate. Were they high or low? Talk about items sold by the pound. Allow kids to bag and weigh the items. After a few trips to the store, little mathematical minds should begin to understand the value of money and how it is used to purchase groceries.

Materials:

Paper
Pen
A trip to the grocery store

Distances

Website:

How far is it?

Address:

http://www.indo.com/distance/

With family and friends spread out all over the world, kids enjoy figuring out where everyone lives in relation to them. Enter names of two cities and this site will find the latitude and longitude of the two places and will then calculate the distance between them. An overview map is also available showing the two places and where they are in relation to each other. Distances are given in miles, kilometers, and nautical miles. Learn the direction you will be heading (for example, East-Northeast) and print out driving directions from your home to your destination.

Activity:

Give each child a measuring tape, divide the class into small groups, and let them measure distances around their home or classroom. Use a variety of units of measurement to find out how far it is from the kitchen to a child's bedroom. Use a measuring tape, an oversized book, a shoe, or the length of a pencil. Is there more than one way to get from the playground to the bathroom? Have them measure both distances and find out which is shorter.

Materials:

Tape measure
Other units of measurement (any household object)

Dollars and Cents

Website:

Kids' Currency Manual

Address:

http://www.northlink.com/~derekb/kidsc.htm

Kids from around the world can create a fortune of funny money by printing out and decorating the dollar pages at this site. Print out currency on different colored papers. Be sure to follow the rules for currency design by being uniform and consistent in design, neat and orderly in drawing. Follow the link to **Community Currencies** and click **National Currency Systems** to read about money and how it is valued and exchanged.

Activity:

Begin to teach your kids the real value of money by playing the *Money Game.* You will need 50 pennies, 6 nickels, 6 dimes, and 1 quarter. Begin by placing the quarter in a prominent place and explaining its value of 25 cents (25 pennies, or 2 dimes and a nickel). Using one die, each player takes a turn rolling, and receives 1 penny for the number rolled. For example, if a player rolls 3, he gets 3 pennies. Each player continues to roll in turn, adding the money together after each roll. If on the next turn the player rolls 4, he gets 4 more pennies, and now has 7 cents. The banker (an adult) trades in 5 pennies for a nickel and explains that the player still has 7 cents (two pennies and a nickel). Continue to play, trading in the coins and explaining equal values (a dime equals 10 pennies, and a nickel equals 5 pennies) until one person has 25 cents. The first person to get 25 cents wins the prized quarter. As the kids begin to understand the value of pennies, nickels, and dimes, you can increase the value of the prize, working your way up to one dollar.

Materials:

50 pennies	8 nickels	6 dimes
1 quarter	Dice	

Forest Fires

Website:

Smokey Bear's
Official Home Page

Address:

http://www.smokeybear.com/

"Only you can prevent forest fires," says Smokey Bear. Smokey helps teach people to take care of the 700 million acres of forests in the United States. Learn how planned, controlled fires help prevent dangerous and destructive wildfires. In **Forest Fun**, discover how people around the world use trees in many different ways. Did you know that rubber for tires comes from a tree? Learn about the many medicines that come from trees. Play the **Campfire Games** to learn **Smokey's Rules for Matches and Campfires**. Try *Memory Buster*, a fun forest memory game, or find the way out of *Smokey's Amazing Forest Maze*. In **Color it Pictures**, children can choose from 41 fun bear pages to color. Learn fun facts about bears on the **Bear Facts** page. Spend some time with Smokey, and be active in preventing fires.

Activity:

Create some neat art with small dry twigs, while you help prevent forest fires. Go for a walk in the woods, and collect dry twigs lying on the ground. Bring the bundles home for decorating vases and picture frames, or constructing a miniature log cabin. Glue the twigs to the sides of a glass jar to create a rustic, one-of-a-kind vase. Glue the twigs in a square or rectangle to make a picture frame. Try constructing a miniature log cabin by binding twigs in rows with glue and string to make walls. Fasten the walls together with glue, and lay twigs across the top as a roof.

Materials:

Twigs	Jar
Glue	String

with Enchanted Learning

Website:

Enchanted Learning Software®
Home Page

Address:

http://www.enchantedlearning.com/Home.html

The educators at **Enchanted Learning** have put together a terrific, extensive website for young children. The site has pages and pages of activities and information on a wide variety of topics, including animals, crafts, geography, and games. There are **Zoom** sections for investigating topics in greater detail. In addition, one of the best features is the **Little Explorers Pictionary**, with links to more than 1,000 other great sites on the Internet. Teachers, parents, and children will all enjoy exploring the many resources at this site. It has won a number of awards, all well-deserved.

Activity:

After all the time that your children have spent on the computer, they need to get up and move! Go outside and play backyard games like Simon Says, Duck Duck Goose, and Hide and Seek. Go for a walk in your neighborhood and have your children make a list of all the things they see along the way.

Learn to Play Chess

Website:
Chess is Fun

Address:
http://www.princeton.edu/~jedwards/cif/chess.html

Kids who learn to play chess often do better in school. So, take advantage of this site to reveal the mysteries of this age-old game of strategic planning and placement. The site offers simple chess instruction, including descriptions and pictures of the board and pieces, the object of the game, the value of the different pieces, and how to keep score. The basic opening strategies of each piece, as well as how and where each piece is allowed to move, are explained in an easy-to-understand format. The site progresses to high-level chess strategy. There are links to virtual chessboards where people of all levels can play others from around the world through their computers.

Bonus site: Chess Dominion Tutorial

http://library.advanced.org/10746/tutorial.html

This site is an interactive chess tutorial that teaches basic chess strategy piece by piece.

Activity:
Let your children design and create their own chess set using materials from around the house. Make the playing board out of a 16-inch by 16-inch piece of plywood or cardboard. Mark lines every 2 inches across the bottom and sides. Use a straight edge to connect the lines, creating 64 squares, and paint in a checkerboard pattern. For playing pieces, use empty film canisters, cut-up egg carton holders, or 1-inch wide wooden dowels cut into pieces 1½ inches in length. Decorate the pieces with markers, paint, fabric, or sequins.

Materials:
      16- x 16-inch piece of cardboard or wood
      Black and white paint
      Pieces (film canisters, cut-up egg carton, wooden dowels)

Mail a Letter

Website:

Celebrate the Century

Address:

http://www.usps.gov/navbar.htm

The mail arrives every day, despite rain, sleet, or snow. How does this happen? Find out by playing the *Post Office Mail Delivery Game* in **Celebrate the Century**. Try delivering the mail using a truck, horse, train, or rocket. How many letters can you get in the mailboxes? At **Mind Over Mail** play the *Stamp Memory Game* by clicking on mail boxes to retrieve identical stamps, or draw and paint your own stamps. The **Collectors Corner** is a great place to begin learning about stamp collecting. Learn how boys and girls can participate in a stamp design contest, where winning designs will be printed on stamps at the turn of the century.

Activity:

Write a letter to a friend down the street, a relative far away, or a pen pal. Allow the kids to put the stamp on the envelope, and explain how that stamp pays for the letter to travel to its destination. Take a trip to the mailbox or post office to mail the letter. Explain how the mail travels around the world. Have your child mail a letter to himself to see how long it takes. To encourage letter writing, set up mailboxes made out of shoeboxes in the classroom or in your home. Encourage your kids to write to each other and to you. Kids can design their own stamps for these letters. The letters make great keepsakes.

Materials:

Crayons
Paper
Envelopes
Stamps
Shoe boxes (for household mailboxes)

Math You Can Eat

Website:

M & M's® Studios

Address:

http://www.m-ms.com/

You can almost smell the chocolate melting in this virtual candy factory. Go for a ride on the monorail, and peek back stage at the M&M's candies. Take the kids on a factory tour to see how the candies are made. If your children like to play with their food, take them to the **Arcade** to experiment with eleven candy coated games. Paint without a mess in **The Art Room**, and be sure to try the confetti and rainbow tools. Help the astronauts pilot a spacecraft in the *Jet Power Game* or try a few rounds of *Mini Golf*. Listen to the M&M's candy stars recite some "way cool" poetry in the **Blue Poetry Cafe**. Order the free cook book in the **Bakery,** so you and your children can prepare tasty new treats.

Activity:

Practice basic math skills by estimating, sorting, counting, and graphing little colored candies or cereal pieces. Pour 25–40 pieces of candy into the bottom of a quart-sized bag. Ask your child to guess how many candies are in the bag, and write the number down. Have your child sort the candies by their color, count how many there are of each color, and write each of those numbers down. Count the total number of candies. Make a graph of the colors using a ruler, and have your child color in the graph using the same color crayon as the candy. Add each of the color numbers together for the grand total. How close was the estimate? Eat the candy together for a tasty finale!

Materials:

Colored candy or cereal
Pencil
Paper
Ruler

Pen Pals

Website:

Penpal Box One

Address:

http://www.ks-connection.org/penpal/recent/B1.html

Hook up with a pen pal from somewhere else in the country or in another part of the world, and learn about life in another place. This site has a long list of children who are eager to exchange e-mail with other children. Each child writes a paragraph about who he is and what he is interested in, then posts it on the site. Your child can either submit his or her own entry, or pick from the ones already posted. For safety reasons, adults will need to monitor any communication with the pen pal.

Activity:

Once your child begins correspondence with a pen pal, research the pen pal's home location (you may use the **How far is it?** website on page 39). Locate an atlas, and trace the outline of where they live. What can you learn about the area and its people. Does your pen pal live in the same country or on a different continent? What is the weather like, is he or she near the beach or the mountains, would you drive to visit them or would it be easier to fly?

Materials:

Atlas
Encyclopedia
Almanac

Public Television on the Web

Website:

PBS Online

Address:

http://www.pbs.org/

PBS Online's Backstage Kids page has all of Public Television's favorite characters linked on one fantastic site. Go for a walk in **Mister Rogers' Neighborhood**, chug down the river with **Theodore Tugboat**, or let your kids go on an adventure and learn about moral courage with *The Children's Book of Virtue*, by William Bennett. Open the **Goodies Bag** and find neat surprises like a coloring book, electronic postcards, or P-Pal Patterns. Learn silly jokes at the **Knock, Knock** page. Snatch the microphone at the **Babble** page and sing your way to fame at *Kid Karaoke*. Explore the science of floating and sinking, the anatomy of the Concorde supersonic airplane, and play with hazardous duty robots at **Nova's Hot Science**. Try the *Pythagorean Puzzle* or *Build a Bridge*. **PBS Kids' TechKnow** teaches the basics about the computer and the Internet.

Activity:

Design a robot. Invent it for a specific purpose such as assembling parts in a factory, walking on the moon, or better yet, cleaning up! Build the robot using recyclable materials, such as laundry detergent containers for the body, old milk jugs for the head, paper towel roles for arms, cereal boxes and tin foil for legs. Use a heavy-duty tape, like mailing tape or masking tape, to hold the robot together. Give children plenty of supplies, and watch as their robots are created.

Materials:

Boxes Milk jugs
Paper roll Foil
Mailing tape

Read, Build, and Create at Look, Learn, and Do

Website:

Look Learn and Do

Address:

http://www.looklearnanddo.com/documents/home.html

This site has a variety of areas from which to choose—projects, books, history, and of course, games. Read *Picnic on a Cloud*, then click on **Learn Some History** to find out how blimps, compasses, and greenhouses were invented. You and your child can find out how to build a windmill, a sailboat, or a blimp at **Build a Project,** and learn fun facts like "Camels have three sets of eyelids" and "Michael Jackson has his own zip code." Play the *Bug Game*, the *Newton Game*, and *Make a Puzzle*. There are also pictures to download and color. A simple, kid-friendly, interesting site.

Activity:

Make a project out of leftover pieces of lumber. With adult help, children can use a hammer and nails to create their own version of almost anything—a dog house, a swimming pool, or a sloping mountainside. Paint the project when the construction is complete. Let their imaginations take over!

Materials:

Lumber scraps
Hammer
Nails
Paint

Reading is Fun

Website:
Calgary Public Library
Summer Reading Game

Address:
http://public-library.calgary.ab.ca/srg98/srg98.htm

Follow a mother whale, Finn, and her baby, Fluke, on their journey through the **Whale of a Tale Reading Game**. There are seven stops along the way, each one filled with jokes and games, information on whales, pirates, and sea creatures. There is also a booklist for different age groups (age 6 and under, ages 7–11, and age 12 and up). You can skip around the site and focus on what interests you, but in order to finish the game, you must take all the quizzes or find items that have been hidden in the pages of the game. When you finish, e-mail the Captain, and your name will be included on a page of **Whale Watchers!** Check out the games page, read about sunken treasure, and find out how whales communicate.

> **Bonus site:** Calgary Public Library games page
>
> http://public-library.calgary.ab.ca/services/gamespl.htm
>
> The Calgary Public Library has several reading games to choose from.

Activity:
Form your own class or family reading club that meets all year long. Read together in a club meeting. Keep a list of all the books that each person reads, and when you reach a goal (for instance ten books each), take everyone to the bookstore or library to replenish your book supply. Choose a book that the whole class or family will enjoy, and read it together.

Materials:
Books

Safety Around Town

Website:

Vince and Larry's Safety City

Address:

http://www.nhtsa.dot.gov/kids/

"You can learn a lot from a dummy." Vince and Larry, the National High-way Traffic Safety Administration's crash test dummies, have their own virtual city on the World Wide Web. At this site, kids can learn about auto, bicycle, and school bus safety by taking a stroll through **Safety City**. Pass the *Safety Challenge*, and have your name engraved on the **High Score Wall of Fame**. There are safety-oriented coloring pages and art supplies to play with in the **Cyber Studio**. Kids can mix their own colors—try yellow and red, blue and yellow. Remember to buckle up before you play *Safety Belt Bingo*, and strap on your head gear before you ride in the *Bicycle Derby*. View some of the crash test dummies' most smashing performances in the **Theater**. Ride your bike through **Safety City**, but look out for the *Danger Zones*!

Activity:

Do a simple bike inspection. Inspect your children's bikes for safety by making sure their bikes have proper reflectors, and checking to make sure the tire pressure isn't too low. Check the brakes to be sure they are working well. Make sure your child's helmet fits properly, since many injuries result from loose fitting helmets. Go for a bike ride around town, through the neighborhood, or in the park. Or review bus safety with your class. Take a field trip to tour through a school bus. Review all safety features of the vehicle, and have students practice sitting properly in their seats. Review safe ways to exit the bus in an emergency.

Scouting for Boys and Girls

Website: Boy Scouts of America®
Address: http://www.bsa.scouting.org/

Learn about scouting and how you can get involved in programs proven to educate, build character, and promote good citizenship, as well as fitness, in young boys. At the **Family Fun** page learn all about semaphore, a way to communicate using two flags. Play with Morse code, learn to use a compass, and experiment with knot tying.

Website: Girl Scouts® of the U.S.A
Address: http://www.girlscouts.org/

Girl Scouts make up a worldwide coalition, 8.5 million girls strong. Come and learn how these special young women raise money selling more cookies than you can imagine. Take the *Online Safety Pledge*. Try cracking the code at the **Brain Games** page or head over to **Just for Girls** to find great sports, science, and tech links for girls. There are even instructions for designing and posting your own web page.

Activity:

Plan a nature scavenger hunt. Go for a hike on a trail, through the park, or around the neighborhood. Make a list of things to pick up along the trail (types of leaves, pine cones, broken twigs, different size rocks, and unfortunately, litter). Bring the list with you, and as your little scouts find items, check the items off the list.

Materials:

Paper   Pen   Bag

The Making of a Book

Website:

HarperCollins® Kids

Address:

http://www.harperchildrens.com/howabook/index.htm

Take a virtual tour with Aliki the cat as she guides you step by step through the book making process. Aliki explains how an idea for a book transforms into a final product, with short and simple explanations of authors, illustrators, and publishers. There are instructions on how to make your own pop-up book, as well as a first-person narrative on book writing called "What they knew first." Play **Switcheroos**, where your child can make aliens, animals, robots or vehicles by exchanging different parts of their bodies. **Wacky Words** asks you to come up with words, then puts them together in a mixed-up, crazy, and often hilarious story. This is a site that encourages reading and writing by showing what fun one can have with words.

Activity:

Have each child write his own story starring friends, favorite characters, or members of the family. Staple several sheets of construction paper together along one side. Encourage the child either to dictate his story to you, or to write down his ideas, with your assistance. Let him draw the illustrations. Have him sign and date the book for future reference.

Materials:

> Construction paper
> Stapler
> Pencil
> Crayons or markers

Why?

Website:

Ask an Expert

Address:

http://www.askanexpert.com/askanexpert/

"Mommy, why is the sky blue?" "Daddy, why are your eyes brown?" "Granny, why does your hair turn gray?" As they grow and learn, kids constantly ask for specific information about the world around them. At **Ask an Expert**, curious children can find some of the answers. Choose from 12 subjects with over 300 websites and e-mail addresses of experts who can answer your questions about topics ranging from the Amish lifestyle to facts about zoo keeping. There are experts on subjects from Astronomy to Zoology. Search the **Categories** page to find a subject related to your wonderkid's question, and the database will provide you with websites and e-mail addresses where you can find the answer.

Activity:

Make your own bubble solution and bubble wand. Mix 1 cup of high quality dish soap with 1 gallon of water and 1 Tbls. of glycerin. Bind a wooden dowel or stick to an empty plastic berry container with garbage ties. Dip the wand into the solution to make a bunch of bubbles. Why do bubbles float through the air? How can you make stronger, longer lasting bubbles? Ask an expert!

Materials:

> Dish Soap
> Glycerin
> Water
> Berry container
> Stick
> Garbage Ties

People have been entertained by television for years, but the advent of the remote control changed television forever. Just as you can use your remote control to change your television channel, website links allow you to change your computer channel. Simply put, websites are many web pages linked together like the pages in a book. These links allow you to go directly to another page within the same site in one click. Links can also connect you to other related websites. The links are usually highlighted in a different color, or are under-lined. Your cursor will change (for instance, from an arrow to a hand) when you point to a link.

Entertainment

Arthur® and D.W.

Website:

Arthur

Address:

http://www.pbs.org/wgbh/pages/arthur

Arthur the Aardvark comes to the web! The creators of Arthur and his friends are committed to encourage kids to develop reading and writing skills, and this site reinforces that commitment. Activities include story writing with tips on how to create good stories, a spot for sending an e-mail message to Arthur, and a kid's art gallery. Children can get details on Arthur's family and friends (nicknames, hobbies, and favorite quotes) as well as a description of every Arthur show that has aired in the past year. Watch your children dance to the theme song written by Ziggy Marley and the Melody Makers. The **Teacher's Corner** has suggestions for lesson plans that reinforce what kids learn from Arthur, such as ways we can help one another, the benefits of having a television-free week, and the importance of good nutrition.

Activity:

Plan a visit to the public library and find out how to get each child their own library card. Pick out an Arthur book that deals with a topic relevant to your class, home, or current issues or problems. The website lists Arthur book titles and themes, and you can even order them from the site. Read, read, read.

Circus
Time

Website:

Ringling Bros.
and Barnum & Bailey^{SM}

Address:

http://ringling.com

"Ladies and gentlemen, boys and girls, children of all ages . . . " This site invites you to peek under the tent at a circus. Enter the **Magnificent Menagerie** to see amazing rare animals and learn fascinating facts. For instance, the world's largest animal, the elephant, is vegetarian and can run up to 25 miles per hour. Bounce on over to *The Torosiants Trampoline Basketball,* and shoot some hoops with Dimitri, Vladimir, and Gregor. Create and print different clown faces. Read about the community in Florida that the circus maintains for its retired animal stars.

Activity:

Host a circus on the playground or in your own back yard. You need a little imagination, a few playmates, and many colors of face paint. Let the kids decide what they want to be—a clown, a tiger, a zebra— (if everyone wants to be a clown, you can host an all-clown circus). Paint the kids' faces with face paint. Soon, you will be surrounded by wacky and wild clowns, tiger faces with orange and black stripes, and zebras with black and white stripes. Give the kids an old hat, and a few hula hoops to use as performance rings. Soon you will hear them shouting, "Ladies and gentlemen, boys and girls . . ."

Materials:

> Face paint (red, black, white, blue, and orange)
> Cotton balls (for the face paint)
> Hula hoops

Create a Story

Website:

Story Creations

Address:

http://www.searsportrait.com/storybook/index.html

Your child can create his or her own personalized storybooks at this site. After entering information about your child (nothing too personal) such as first name, favorite food, color, and a friend's name, choose from many stories, including holiday tales from Hanukkah, Kwanza Day, Thanksgiving, Christmas, and Valentine's Day, and adventure stories where your children are the heroes. There is *A Day in the Park, A Trip to Yellowstone, Fun in the Snow, Dinosaur Adventure,* and even *A New Baby Coming Home.* Fasten the stories into paper folders to create a personal book collection. Best of all, your children star in every story. The kids will have you traveling back to this site again and again, until their personalized story library is complete.

Activity:

Everybody in the classroom or family can participate in this interactive story game. Pick a topic for a story, such as space, the forest, or a soccer game . . . anything you like! Adults start by making up a sentence and each person in the room takes a turn adding a sentence, leaving his own definitive imprint upon the story. You never know how the story will unfold. The story may begin as a mission in outer space, then unravel into silly 5 year-old wacky humor. This is a great game to play in the car. Tape-record your stories for some hilarious playbacks!

Materials:

Tape recorder (optional)

Cruella, Pocahontas, and Hercules— Disney® on the Web

Website:

Disney.com—The Web Site for Families

Address:

http://www.disney.com/

For the Disney fanatic, this site is a dream come true. It is filled with games, stories, and puzzles, as well as links to movies, software, videos, and Walt Disney World. There are member fees for a variety of services, but there is plenty to try for free. Create personalized stories with *Mickey's Alphabet* and practice spelling with *Donald Dunking*. Give Cruella, the evil vixen from 101 Dalmatians, a desperately needed makeover by clicking on her eyes, nose, mouth, and hair. Play *Mermaid to Order* by fitting shapes into their proper spots. Animated cartoon strips can be found under the **Comic Spot,** and **Pocahontas' Print Studio** is worth a look as well. Be sure to read the explicit instructions Disney has provided about the specific technology you will need to get the best results from their site.

Activity:

Teach your children how to make a cartoon. Have each child make up their own cartoon characters and have them draw the very first comic strip using these characters. Show them how to make dialogue balloons and how to split the cartoon into four frames. Help with the words if needed.

Materials: Paper and pencil

Dr. Seuss and Friends

Website:

Dr. Seuss's Seussville℠

Address:

http://www.randomhouse.com/seussville/

Enter the wonderful world of Dr. Seuss and interact with the Cat in the Hat, Horton, the Lorax, Sam-I-Am, and many of your children's other Seussville friends. Play *Slyvester McBean's Sneetch Belly Game, Hooray for Diffendoofer Game,* and the *Lorax's Save the Trees Game.* Go on *Horton's Who Hunt* and print out *Connect the Dots* pages and *The Cat's Hat Maze.* Access the **More Fun** section and click on *Green Eggs and Ham.* When you get there, work the picture scramble, click on **Crafts for Eggheads**, and go to an *Egg-citing Activity*, where you can print out a placemat complete with outlines showing the correct positions for eating utensils (an easy way to introduce a little etiquette lesson). Read a short biography of Dr. Seuss, written with children in mind.

Activity:

Make green eggs and ham. Whisk up a batch of scrambled eggs and add a few drops of green food coloring. Add a side of ham and you are ready to be Sam-I-Am.

Materials:

Scrambled eggs
Green food coloring
Ham

Luke, Han, and Leia

Website:

Star Wars Imperial Center

Address:

http://www.imperialcenter.com/center2.html

This is an awesome site for the Star Wars fan. Click on the shuttle and enter Coruscant space and the glorious heart of the Empire. The **Multimedia** section has spy footage of Rebel and Imperial activities, pictures of both Imperial and Rebel ships, audio clips and MIDI music from the Star Wars films, as well as columns written by Star Wars fans. Go to **Top Ten Lists** and find out the *Top Ten Reasons Not to Join the Empire, Not to Hang Around the Jabba's Palace,* and the *Top Ten Stars Wars Insults,* to name a few. Take the trivia contest, get technical data on all the ships in the galaxy, and investigate the **Secret Files**. Learn fascinating facts about the Force, Luke, Han, Leia, and the Evil Empire.

Activity:

Make up your own Star Wars trivia game. Every player comes up with ten trivia questions and writes them down on a piece of paper. Each player then switches questions with another player. Adults may need to help with reading and writing the questions. Give one point for every correct answer and see who truly has the Force on their side.

Materials:

Pen and paper

Puppet Parade

Website:

Welcome to Stage Hand
Puppets Activity Page

Address:

http://www3.ns.sympatico.ca/onstage/puppets

Learn to make your own puppets, write your own plays, even publish your creative works at the **Online Puppet Theater**. The **Scrap Puppets** page teaches children to make puppets out of household items, including old socks and newspaper. Discover puppet performance secrets from the Professor on how ventriloquists throw their voice, and soon unexpected objects around the house may begin to talk. At the **Patterns** page, kids can download and print out patterns for hundreds of puppets—kitten and monkey puppets, dancing puppets on a string, and origami stick puppets.

> **Bonus site:** Puppets are People Too
> http://members.xoom.com/Puppetry
> Information on basic puppetry techniques and starting a puppet troupe.

Activity:

Create a theater for your little puppet masters to play with. After a visit to this site, your kids have enough information for making neat puppets. Find a cardboard box big enough for a child to crawl in or hide behind and cut a stage (a square) out of the front of the box. Cut a flap in the back of the box for crawling in and out. Make a curtain for the theater by taping 2 panels of lightweight fabric above the stage opening. If you don't have a big box, hang up a sheet in a doorway. The kids can crawl behind the sheet and stick their puppets through the slit by the door frame. Get ready for the show as kids enjoy performing for a captive audience.

Materials:

Large Box	Sheet
Fabric	Scissors

Rug Rats

Website:

Rug Rats Preschool Home Page

Address:

http://www.mnsinc.com/osfan/index.htm

Who would have thought you could learn so much from the Rug Rats? This site has mazes, recipes for "yucky" stuff to play with, puzzles, and more. **Animal Alphabet Stories** and **Tweety's Sign Language** page are stand-outs. On the Animal Alphabet Stories page, your child learns fascinating facts about a different animal for every letter of the alphabet. After you investigate animals A to Z, go to Tweety's Sign Language page where you and your children can learn how to finger spell by following clear and detailed illustrations. This site draws you in with the lure of cartoon characters, but keeps you interested with quality activities and information.

Activity:

Begin to learn sign language by practicing finger spelling each child's name. Talk about different ways people communicate (different languages, a baby's cry, dogs barking) and why it is important to be able to communicate in many different ways. See how many languages the children can name.

Sesame Street®

Website:

Sesame Street Central

Address:

http://www.ctw.org/sesame/

Join Elmo, Ernie, and the rest of the gang from one of Public Television's most popular shows as they continue to entertain and educate your children. Your children can help decide what happens next in online storybooks like *Zoo Who?*, where kids can create original animals out of a variety of animal body parts. Other storybooks include *High Noon, Thanks for the Memories,* and *The Yucky Letter M.* You can print out coloring and activity pages for offline fun, or stay online and enter the activity arena. The activities are divided into five categories—**Dot to Dot, Fit the Shape, Hidden Numbers, Hidden Letters,** and **1 of These Things**. Within these categories are numerous games, for example *Prairie Dawn Builds a Dollhouse, Grover of Arabia,* and *Toss a Salad with Cookie Monster.*

Activity:

Play a simple alphabet game with your children. Ask them to name a word, or an animal, or a food that begins with the letter A. Proceed with letter B, C, D and so on. For older children, ask them to name a word that ends with a certain letter. Go in alphabetical order with younger children, but mix up the letters for older kids. Make the game more challenging by narrowing the category; for example, name a place, or a song.

Snoopy® and the Peanuts® Gang

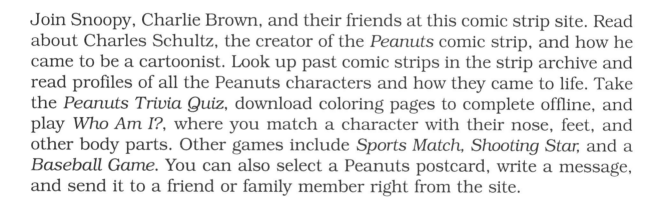

Website:

Welcome to Snoopy.com

Address:

http://www.unitedmedia.com/comics/peanuts/index.html

Join Snoopy, Charlie Brown, and their friends at this comic strip site. Read about Charles Schultz, the creator of the *Peanuts* comic strip, and how he came to be a cartoonist. Look up past comic strips in the strip archive and read profiles of all the Peanuts characters and how they came to life. Take the *Peanuts Trivia Quiz*, download coloring pages to complete offline, and play *Who Am I?*, where you match a character with their nose, feet, and other body parts. Other games include *Sports Match, Shooting Star,* and a *Baseball Game.* You can also select a Peanuts postcard, write a message, and send it to a friend or family member right from the site.

Activity:

Teach your children how to kick a football. The children can reenact Charlie Brown's mission to kick the ball, but don't yank it away like Lucy does! An adult can hold the ball and let each child practice kicking it. Show her how to stand the football up by tilting it back slightly.

Materials:

Football

Winnie–the–Pooh®

Website:

Winnie-the-Pooh® and Friends—
An Expotition

Address:

http://www.worldkids.net/pooh/

Enter the 100-Aker Wood and visit friends familiar to you from your own childhood as well as your children's. Expotition means a special adventure. At Pooh's expotition, you can travel to the 100-Aker Wood for adventure after adventure. Go to **Kanga's House, Pooh's Trap for Heffalumps, Tigger's Bouncing Place,** or any one of the other twenty places to visit. There are games to play, video clips to watch, and songs to learn. After you have exhausted the expotition, download some **Coloring Book** pages, and check out the cool stuff at the **Readers'** pages.

Activity:

Plan a picnic in the Hundred-Acre Wood. Let the children help prepare the food. Be sure to bring along bread, honey and a few Winnie the Pooh storybooks to share after you have finished your meal.

Materials:

Bread and honey
Picnic food
Winnie-the-Pooh® storybooks

Everyone loves to get mail, and now it is easier than ever to send and receive mail when you use your computer. All you need to do is find out what your friends' e-mail addresses are, and you have instant pen pals. Type in your friend's address, write your message, and hit the send button. Most mail systems have address books, as well as forward, reply, and attach commands. There are also search engines such as http://www.infospace.com to help you find a friend's address if you don't have it.

Just for Fun

Adventure with Nikolai®

Website:

Nikolai® and Neow Neow
Under the Big Top

Address:

http://www.nikolai.com/

Visit two lovable and adventurous storybook characters at Nikolai and Neow Neow's cyber playground. Read books from their bookshelf and help to complete their stories for a new and exciting outcome each time. Your little authors can star in their own personalized stories or they can submit original stories in **The Attic**. In the **Joke Book**, find new jokes sent in by kids around the world. There are plenty of activities to print out in the **Rumpus Room**, including origami printouts for seals, birds, and penguins. Find new recipes, and write on a virtual chalkboard in the **Toy Ches**t. Fly over to the **Games Galaxy** to play cool games like *Ask the Fish, Pirate Panic,* or *Domineows*. The **ABCD's of Learning** offers math, language arts, and science activities and lessons to print out or complete online.

Activity:

Create a mini-adventure on the playground or in your driveway by drawing mazes with sidewalk chalk. Parents and children can design their best mazes. Draw a jungle maze with plenty of twists and turns (don't forget to hide a cheetah in the trees). Draw a city street maze with lots of dead ends (watch out for the parked cars). Try finding the way out of each other's maze. How many times do you have to turn around? For fast action fun, keep time with a stopwatch. After you master a maze, try it blind folded.

Materials:

Sidewalk chalk

Beanie Baby Pals

Website:

Ty—The Official Home of
the Beanie Babies®

Address:

http://www.ty.com

Is the Beanie Baby craze dying? Not in our homes, but at least now you
can find Beanie Babies without following the UPS truck around. For those
kids who just can't get enough of the little beanbag animals, this site has
it all. Sign the **Guestbook**, check out the **Attic Treasures Collection**, and
take a look at the **Dog House,** the **Kitty Klub,** and the **Bear Den**. You get
the picture—this is Beanie Baby heaven.

Activity:

Choose a habitat that is appropriate for bear Beanie Babies. Use
shoeboxes to make a den and decorate it with twigs and other leaves.
Think about where the bears would get their food and water.

Materials:

Boxes
Markers
Fabric scraps
Bits of nature
Shoeboxes

Freebies

Website:

Free Stuff—The Ultimate Source for Bargain Lovers!

Address:

http://www.ppi-free.com/freekid.htm

All kids love to receive mail, and on this site you can find free offers for almost anything. Choose from a variety of subject categories like angels, Christmas, crafts, magazines, and sewing. Offers include free sample copies of magazines, booklets written for children about eating properly, craft ideas, and gift projects. Some offers have postage and handling charges. You can also join an e-mail list for updates of free stuff.

Activity:

While you and your children are busy waiting for your free stuff to arrive, collect a box of your own "free stuff" to give away to charity. Enlist the children's help in sorting through outgrown clothing, little used toys, and children's magazines that you are finished with. Talk about the importance of remembering to share with those less fortunate than you.

Fun
and
Games

Website:

KidsCom: Play Smart, Stay Safe and Have Fun!

Address:

http://www.kidscom.com/

This is an extensive site with a wide variety of activities, games to play, and cool stuff. Your class can send a message to Presidents and world leaders regarding their concerns, they can make new friends via a pen pal exchange, or they can enter a chat room to talk with other kids with similar interests. Most children will be drawn to the games, which are fun and not complicated. Try the *Turkey Drop, Iggey and Rasper's Internet Safety Game,* and *Concentration.* Solve the puzzles and experiment with the disguise maker. Be prepared to spend some time here.

Activity:

Play Concentration with a real deck of cards. Use Old Maid cards or any other deck from a child's card game. Spread out all the cards face down on the floor or table. Take turns flipping over two cards at a time to find a matching pair. Each time you match a pair, remove it from the table. This is a timeless memory game for all ages to enjoy.

Materials:

Deck of cards from a child's card game

Games, Activities, Fun, and Education

Website:

Bonus.com

Address:

http://www.bonus.com

This site consistently makes the lists of top ten websites and you will soon know why. Click on **Parents and Teachers First Time Tour** for an introduction to the site. You can then choose from **Young Kids** (preschoolers) or **Advanced Kids** (kindergarten and up). There are hundreds of things to do at this site, ranging from simple puzzles to complicated brain games. The main menu offers 5 different areas to explore—**Play, Imagine, New Fun, Explore,** and **Color**. Within each area are numerous pages to investigate. For example, in Play, children can choose from 13 different categories of games (arcade, sports, word, board), then select individual games from within these categories. The games are first rate, and the activities capture your attention. You might want to bookmark this site and come back again and again.

Activity:

Make your own crossword puzzle. Have the children chose 10 words, and with a piece of graph paper, help them figure out how to make the words intersect at common letters. Once they have completed the graphing of the puzzle, number the words and have them come up with clues. Then make a new puzzle outline, and write the clues on that piece of paper. Have each child give it to a friend or family member to solve. This is fun to do with a theme as well, for example back to school (apples, teacher, bus, pencil) or food (pizza, chips, banana, cookie).

Materials:

Graph paper   Pencil

Join Club Theo

Website:

Club Theo.com

Address:

http://www.clubtheo.com/letsplay/index.html

Games, stories, recipes, and fun facts make up this entertaining website for young children. Enter **Dallas' Way to Play** and begin with the **Bike Puzzle**, where you help Theo put his bicycle back together again. Go bowling with coconut balls at the *Sliding Puzzle*, learn to count to ten in Japanese, Russian, and Spanish at the *Numbers Game*, and build an original masterpiece at the *Block Game*. Read: *I'm Five!*, *No Wonder We're So Confused*, and *Marbles and Gumballs* at **Theo's World of Words**, then try out the *Wacky Word Games*. Experiment with the recipes in **Dewey's Global Munchies,** and find out which part of the world your favorite foods come from.

Activity:

After learning numbers in different languages, play a game of Funny Numbers. Take a deck of cards and remove the jack, queen, and king cards from the deck. The aces become ones. Shuffle the remaining cards, and distribute them to the players. Take turns turning over one card at a time. The first player turns over a card and calls out the number on the card in as many languages as he can. Proceed with each player turning over his cards, one at a time, until they are all gone. Give one point for every correct answer. The player with the most points at the end of the game is the winner.

Materials:

Deck of cards

Learning with Legos®

Website:

Lego.com

Address:

http://www.lego.com

Did you know that there are 102,981,500 different ways to combine six 8-stud Lego pieces of the same color? Bone up on Lego trivia, from the company's inception in 1932 to the latest and greatest facts and figures. Play the interactive games: *A Day at the Seaside, The Quest for the Ruby,* and *UFO Blast Off,* as well as *Duplo Turn N Match* or *Belville Turn N Match.* Explore the **Legoland Parks**, including the new park in Carlsbad, California.

Activity:

Build, build, build. Lego pieces come in many shapes, sizes, and forms, as the website will show you. If you do not already own Lego sets, invest in a basic set and join the children in creating buildings, creatures, and vehicles from different-colored plastic bricks. Try making a car or a house, then graduate to something more complicated, such as a hospital or a make-believe animal.

Materials:

Lego or other plastic building bricks

Name that Name

Website:

What's In A Name?

Address:

http://bnf.parentsoup.com/babyname/

On a day when you do not have much spare time, log on and research each child's name. They love to see their names in print, to find out the meaning of their names, and to know where the name originated. Chances are, you will be researching not only their names, but those of neighbors, friends, and classmates as well. This is especially nice for those kids who have somewhat unusual names that are not found on mini-license plates, key chains, or notepads. Later, when the kids are gone, check out other great resources for education, child rearing, and family issues in **Parent Soup**, the main site for this link.

Activity:

Tell your children how their names were chosen, why they were named after a family member, other names that were in the running but didn't make it to the birth certificate. Talk about why names were eliminated and how long it took to come up with their names. These are the stories that give children their identity and solidify family ties. Have your children write their names, then mix up the letters to see what other words can be spelled using the same letters in a different order.

Materials:

Pencil and paper

Play with the Berenstain Bears®

Website:

Activities for Learning and Fun

Address:

http://www.berenstainbears.com/learnfun.html

Bears don't hibernate in this virtual den. At this site, kids learning to use the computer can practice using their mouse to find their way through some tricky mazes. Print a calendar, a coloring book, or bear paper dolls. Kids can actually create their own bear family by printing out the Berenstain Bears paper dolls (Mamma, Papa, Brother, and Sister). Each of the bears has six different wardrobes to print and decorate. The **Actual Factual's Fabulous Factoids** page has interesting trivia on crawling fish, whopper whales, itty-bitty bats, and positively platypus. Finish up by trying to decode the mystery message.

Activity:

Create paper dolls of your entire family, including pets if you have any. Glue pictures of each family member onto a sturdy piece of cardboard. Cut out the person and mount it with tape to an empty film canister, so the cut-out picture stands upright. From a shoebox, construct and decorate a house for the family to live in. Play house with your kids. Try reversing roles in the family. Have some tea with the paper doll bear family.

Materials:

Pictures of your family members Shoe box
Cardboard Empty film canisters
Glue and tape

Race Track Fun

Website:

Hot Wheels® Raceway

Address:

http://www.hotwheels.com/speedcity/speedcity.html

Race over to this Internet pit stop for some high-speed action. New racers can register with a nickname (no personal information required) at the **Department of Motor Vehicles** or check out **Speed City** as a visitor. Play *Capture the Flag*, where kids can design, construct, and test different race-tracks. In the **Raceway**, you can challenge youth from other countries in a race for the prized *Hot Wheels Racing Cup*. Try navigating off-road vehicles through the *Swamp Stomp*, *Desert Drag*, or *Rocky Mountains*. Watch out for the rough terrain and trees in your path! In **Speed City's Post Office**, kids can send all kinds of Hot Wheels e-mail postcards to their friends.

Activity:

Teach your boys and girls science while they play with toy cars. Demonstrate the law of gravity by placing two pieces of track or cardboard at different angles—one steep and one just slightly inclined. Race two similar toy cars down the tracks. Which car goes faster? Why? Gravity drags the cars down the track. Discuss gravity and how it affects our life and play. Try throwing a ball or jumping on a trampoline—you couldn't do it without gravity.

Materials:

> Little race cars
> Track

Take–out Pizza

Website:

Tony's Pizza factory

Address:

http://www.tonys.com/mainpage.htm

Pizza reigns supreme for kids, and now they can become true pizza connoisseurs. Check out the **Pizza Hall of Fame**, and read about Tony and his family in **Tony's Story.** Have your child make her own pizza in the **Pizza Lab** and send it via e-mail to her friends. Play *Pizza Match-up*, work a pizza puzzle, and try your hand at *Pizza Blasters*. Read funny jokes and stories in the **Breakroom** and submit your own for inclusion in the site.

Activity:

Make a pizza! Slice English muffins in half and give the children each enough tomato sauce to spread on top. Provide shredded mozzarella cheese, sliced-up veggies, and other favorite toppings. Let them design their own pizza, then put it in the toaster oven until the cheese bubbles. Children love to create in the kitchen, and this is a fun and easy culinary project.

Materials:

English muffins
Tomato sauce
Mozzarella cheese
Sliced vegetables and other toppings
Toaster oven

Treasure Hunt

Website:

Cyberjacques

Address:

http://www.cyberjacques.com/

Surf the web at high tide, and ride the waves into this oceanfront arcade full of fun and frolic. The site is packed with ten entertaining cybersea games. The goal of each is to complete tasks that will uncover a secret password, which changes every week. Kids can toss pies at Pete while avoiding hungry fish, or use their mouse to recognize numbers in a game of connect-the-dots. Can your little pirate avoid walking the plank in the *Plank Jumper*? The geometric puzzle *Tantagram* is great for beginning problem solvers. Other games include *Memory Matching*, *Hangman*, *Simon Says*, and *What's Inside*. All of these games will keep your little sailors surfing back again and again.

Activity:

Send your small starfish on a treasure hunt! Make up a paper trail (index cards or pieces of paper) of clues and plant them around the house or classroom. Each clue should indicate where the next clue can be found. For early readers, write simple messages like "dog house" (if the next clue is in the doghouse) or glue cereal to a card if the next note is hidden in the pantry, and so on. For non-readers, paste or draw pictures on cards. You can cut pictures out of magazines. Plan the hunt to cover a large area, such as the playground or around the house. Hide up to 10 different notes. The last clue should lead to the treasure. Treasure can be anything that brings a smile, such as homemade jewelry, baseball cards, candy, or a favorite misplaced toy.

Materials:

Pen   Paper   Treasure

Traveling to new and different places can be both fun and exciting, but to figure out where you are going, you need a set of traveling tools. The most important of these tools is a map to show you how to get to your destination and what connections you need to make your trip go smoothly. Think of your browser as your tool to connect you to the sites you wish to explore on the world wide web. The two most popular browsers are Netscape Navigator and Microsoft Explorer, both of which are easy to use and master. Have fun on your Internet adventures!

Geography and Travel

Africa

Website:

Kids Zone: Discover Africa

Address:

http://www.afroam.org/children/discover/discover.html

Where exactly is Mozambique? What is the capital of Zimbabwe? What kinds of animals live in Mali? Discover the countries of Africa and the people who live there on this educational and fun-filled site. Look up interesting facts about Africa's geography and people, identify countries in the different regions of the continent, and play a game to test your knowledge of African animals. There are puzzles to work, word scrambles to solve, and a great *Black History Quiz* to complete. Finish up by reading and discussing African myths and fables like *Anansi the Spider*, *The Rabbit, The Elephant and the Whale*, and *Why Crocodile has a Rough Back*. A wonderful site about a fascinating part of the world.

Activity:

Make an animal mask. Take a large white paper plate and have your child cut out eyeholes for his mask. Let him paint the mask to suit the animal he would like to be, such as a golden lion or a striped tiger. Once the paint has dried, decorate the mask with construction paper cut outs for the ears, nose, and mouth, or cut out the mouth opening from the plate. Attach yarn for a lion's mane or bits of brown tufts for the top of a giraffe's head. When the mask is complete, use a hot glue gun to attach a craft or ice cream stick to the bottom of the mask.

Materials:

Paint	Large paper plate
Scissors	Construction paper
Yarn	Sequins, buttons, or other decorations
Hot glue gun	Craft or ice cream stick

Amazing Alaska

Website:
Alaska From a Kid's
Point of View

Address:
http://www.tqjunior.advanced.org/3784/

Ever wonder how to keep warm in Alaska? What do people do in all that
ice and snow? Sports, adventure stories, fashions (layers, layers, and layers), and other Alaskan facts are all on this kid-designed web page. Put
together by four home-schooled children, this site lets you in on all you
ever wanted to know about Alaska. Forget the average daily temperature—
let's hear about the time the moose ended up in your kitchen! These kids
share all the details of their lives and introduce your children to bunny
boots, neckgaiters, and handwarmers. Move on to information about igloos
and the midnight sun, then read about dog mushing and ice fishing. Go
along on a whitewater adventure, a bear scare, and whale watching. A
great site by kids, for kids.

> **Bonus site:** Alaska Kids Zone
>
> http://www.juneau.com/kids
>
> Check out the variety of Alaskan links, links to other great kids' stuff, and
> a listing of parents' resources.

Activity:
Look up Alaska in the atlas, and figure out how far away it is from
your home. How could you get there? How long would it take? What
would you do once you arrived? What should you pack? What kinds
of animals would you hope to see? Ask your children to draw a picture of what they think Alaska looks like.

Materials:

Atlas	Paper	Markers or crayons

Cameras Around the World

Website:

Around the World in 80 Clicks

Address:

http://www.steveweb.com/80clicks/frontpages/FrontContent.html

Travel around the world in 80 clicks of your mouse. This site features up-to-date photographs from web cameras in cities around the world. The tour begins and ends in New York City. On the way, visit Boston, Ontario, Dublin, Krakow, London, Hong Kong, Sydney, Paris, Capetown, and other cities. View the Kremlin in Moscow, the Wailing Wall in Jerusalem, or South Beach in Miami. Tour at your own pace because each time you log on, the tour resumes in the city where you logged off. When you successfully complete your journey around the globe, register with the travelogue to become a recognized cyber-world traveler.

Activity:

Put together and play a game of travel bingo. Before the next family or class trip, cut out twenty-five pictures of things you may see along the way. If you are flying to a big city, you should see a plane, pilot, big buildings, and taxis. If you are driving through the country, you should see cows, corn, haystacks, and barns. Place the cut-out pictures on a piece of corrugated cardboard in grids of 5 down and 5 across. When your child sees the real person, place, or thing that is pictured on the board, cover the picture with a self-stick note. Five in a row, you've got Bingo! Count the total you find on your journey. You can use different colored notes if more than one person is playing.

Materials:

Pictures of sights you may see
9- x 11-inch piece of cardboard
Glue
Colored self-stick notes

Camp Out in Ontario Parks

Website:
Welcome to Ontario Parks

Address:
http://www.mnr.gov.on.ca/MNR/parks/index.html

Explore and discover a beautiful Canadian park system where you can plan your next vacation, go on tours of the parks, follow Algonquin canoe routes, and of course, visit the **Park Arcade**. At the Arcade you can take a *Magic Canoe Ride,* go on a *Bug Hunt,* or go on the *Bon Echo Park Quicktime VR Tour.* Read park legends and lore, see and listen to wildlife sights and sounds, and take the trivia quiz. A great outdoors site.

Activity:
Pretend you are going on a camping trip. Make a list of the things you will need to bring, the animals you hope to see, the activities you would like to try. Plan a camp-out in the backyard or set up a makeshift tent in the classroom. Eat hot dogs and roast marshmallows for s'mores. At naptime or bedtime, roll out the sleeping bags and tell a not-too-scary ghost story. Get out your flashlight in case you need to see in the dark.

Materials:
Tent or blankets to make a "tent"
Sleeping bags
Flashlight

Explore with National Geographic®

Website:

National Geographic.com/kids

Address:

http://www.nationalgeographic.com/kids/

Welcome to the wonderful world of National Geographic. Log onto this site when you have lots of time, because it could be tough to tear your kids away. Read exciting narratives about the Great Chicago Fire, the sinking of the Titanic. and other momentous historical events. Take the **Shark Surfari**, and after your child answers the questions correctly, you and your child can print out a *Cool Certificate* to announce their expertise. Enter the **Fantastic Forest**, explore a fortress, and save a Siberian tiger from extinction. Find out why clouds float, why snow stays on mountain-tops, and why the wind blows. There are numerous trivia quizzes, games and jokes (for example, Q: What are cows doing when they're dancing? A: Making milk shakes). The list goes on and on.

Activity:

Once you have discovered why the wind blows, make a set of wind chimes. Begin with a base, such as a wire coat hanger. Attach pieces of thick string or twine to the coat hanger, then decide what you will use for your 'chimes.' Seashells are one option. Adults can attach the seashells to the string either by drilling a small hole in the top of the shell and stringing the twine through the hole, or by using a hot glue gun. Hang the chimes up by the hook of the hanger, and wait for the wind to come along and make music!

Materials:

Wire coat hanger	Music makers, such as sea shells
String or twine	Drill or hot glue gun *(adults only)*

Great Expeditions

Website:
Discovery Channel Online

Address:
http://www.discovery.com/

Journey on exhilarating expeditions, explore recent discoveries, and unmask some interesting animals with the **Discovery Channel Online**. At the **Discovery School** your kids can enter their grade level and search the database for cool, age-appropriate information on their favorite topics. Check out new TV programs on the history of science, astronomy, and ancient Egypt. Travel to the **Animal Planet** and participate in *World Animal Day*. Read online stories about life as a shark, or a gorilla, and visit the *Crocodile Hunter* down under in Australia. Climb aboard the 80-foot animal rescue truck that was created to help animals during a natural disaster. Watch sharks, whales, and orangutans in their natural habitats on live animal cams. Play **Mind Games** and see if you can *Name that Plane*, or find *The Missing Link*.

Activity:

Demonstrate how fossils form. Place small plastic bugs or animals into a clear plastic container. Mix 3 or 4 different colors of water by mixing food coloring and water in individual cups. Pour one color of water into the clear container, covering only the feet of the animals, and freeze. After the first layer is frozen, pour in another thin layer of a different color water and freeze. Repeat, until the animals are covered by 1 inch of ice. Explain to your kids how the different colored ice layers represent distinct layers of sedimentary rock that form over time (millions of years). Allow the kids to dig out their "fossils."

Materials:

Clear container	Small plastic animals
Water	Food coloring

Lighthouses of the World

Website:

Linda's Lighthouse Page

Address:

http://www.umcc.ais.org/~lsa

The cry "Land ho!" prevents a ship from being wrecked on a reef and saves her sailors from great peril. Keepers of the lighthouses work long and often lonely hours to protect ships and sailors by guiding them safely away from hazards, even when visibility is low. This website introduces your children to lighthouses and their keepers around the world. View pictures and read about the history of ancient and modern lighthouses. Find out which lighthouse is the tallest, which is the oldest, and which protects ships from the most threatening dangers.

> **Bonus site:** Legendary Lighthouses
>
> http://www.pbs.org/legendarylighthouses
>
> Read the history, and view pictures of fascinating lighthouses from this PBS series on lighthouses.

Activity:

Build a model boat. You need a flat piece of wood about 1 foot long and 6 inches wide. Glue a dowel in the center as a mast. Make a sail by cutting a rectangle from a scrap of fabric, cardboard, or plastic. Thread the sail onto the mast on the top and bottom. Sail your boat in the bathtub or take it to a pond. If you sail it in a lake be sure to tie a string to it so you can reel it back. Talk about boats and why they are important. Toys travel on boats across the ocean. People use boats to fish, to explore, and for entertainment. What can your boat do?

Materials:

Flat piece of wood	Dowel or stick
Fabric for sail	Glue

Maps, Maps, Maps

Website:

TerraServer

Address:

http://terraserver.microsoft.com/

Welcome to the biggest online world imagery database. Here you can look at your neighborhood from outer space or get an aerial shot of your favorite park. This Microsoft site allows you to choose any spot on our planet and view high resolution images from the U.S. Geological Survey's aerial photography and the Spin 2 satellite, a joint U.S.-Russian information project. Have fun! Look up your hometown, your school, or a friend's house. See what's going on around the corner or at Grandma's house. The pictures allow you to zoom in on specific areas. It sure looks different from up there, doesn't it? Check out the **Famous Places** page to view prominent places from around the world such as Venice, Italy, the Grand Canyon, or the island of Alcatraz off the coast of San Francisco.

Activity:

Create planet Earth and decorate it to look like Earth from outer space. Cover a round balloon in papier-mâché. Cut newspaper into 2-inch strips and dip into mixture (2 cups water, 1 cup flour, 1 Tbls. of glue). Cover the balloon in three layers and allow it to dry. Cut a slit and remove the balloon. Paint the Earth blue to demonstrate that the Earth is covered mostly with water. Paint and label the continents, using a globe or atlas as a guide.

Materials:

Balloon	Newspaper (cut in 1-inch strips)
Flour	Glue
Water	Paint
Globe or atlas	

Mount Rushmore

Website:

The Official Mount Rushmore
Home Page

Address:

http://www.state.sd.us/tourism/rushmore/index.htm

Use this site to read about the *four most famous guys in rock*—learn the history of Mt. Rushmore! View photos of the mountain before and after the sculpting at this well-written and information-laden site. Find out what motivated sculptor Gutzon Borglum to drill into a 6,200-foot mountain to form the heads of the four presidents, and create his *Shrine to Democracy.* Discover how this amazing feat was achieved and the obstacles that occurred along the way. Get park information, watch video clips of the Fourth of July celebration (downloading takes some time), and look at the park's photo album.

Activity:

Make your own sculpture out of baking soda play clay. Place 2 cups of baking soda, 1 cup of cornstarch and 1¼ cups water in a saucepan. Adults should stir the mixture over low heat for about 15 minutes. Remove from the heat, but keep stirring. When the mixture feels like mashed potatoes, it is ready for sculpting. Older children can try to make their own Mt. Rushmore by sculpting members of their family, while younger children will enjoy playing with the clay. The clay will dry in about 12 hours and will then be ready for painting if you like.

Materials:

> 2 cups baking soda
> 1 cup cornstarch
> 1¼ cups water
> Saucepan
> Paint and brushes (optional)

The County Fair

Website:

Michigan Department of
Agriculture Kidz Corner

Address:

http://www.mda.state.mi.us/kids/countyfair/index.html

Spend a day at the Michigan county fair, compliments of the Michigan Department of Agriculture's Kidz Corner. Find out how crops are grown and maintained, and what products ultimately are made from these crops. Clear and interesting photographs accompany the crop descriptions. Join Booster Rooster in making and baking Michigan Apple Crisp and learn about handling food safely at the same time. Play a matchmaker game, and read interesting life stories written by kids who live in Michigan, such as *Rachel's Story: My Life on a Michigan Dairy Farm*. There is also a section on different animals that you may find at the fair.

Activity:

Use old paper grocery bags to make apple print wrapping paper. Cut a brown paper bag along the side and along the bottom panel. Remove and discard the bottom panel, and open up the bag so that it lays flat. Cut an apple in half lengthwise, and dip it into red paint. Press the apple on the paper to make pretty apple prints. Use the paper to wrap gifts for the holidays or for a birthday.

Materials:

> Brown paper bags
> Scissors
> Apple
> Red paint

The Ecuadorian Amazon

Website:

Amazon Interactive

Address:

http://www.eduweb.com/amazon.html

There is a lot to explore at this site. Learn the origins of the word Amazon, click on a map of the world to locate the Amazon region in South America, and compare the average annual rainfall in the Amazon to the rainfall in the area where you live. Read about the Mestizos who live there and how they make a living. Research planting and crop strategies designed to insure income for the local community now, as well as conservation of the land for the future. Play the *Ecotourism Simulation Game*, where you make choices about agriculture and tourism in order to try to balance income and preservation of the land and community. A nice geography site about a crucial part of the world.

Activity:

The Amazon is home to a wide variety of birds. To find out what kinds of birds live in your area, attract them by making a birdfeeder. Find a large pinecone, or if not readily available buy one at a craft store, and screw an eyehook to the top. Spread peanut butter on the pinecone, then roll the pinecone in birdseed. Run picture-hanging wire or thick twine through the eyehook and tie to a tree branch in the backyard or outside your classroom window. You will not wait long for the birds to arrive!

Materials:

Pinecone	Picture-hanging wire or thick twine
Peanut butter	Eye hook
Birdseed	

The Great Wall of China

Website:

China: Beyond the Great Wall

Address:

http://www.uncletai.com/china/china.html

Begin with wonderful photographs of The Great Wall and other impressive sights in China, including the Imperial Summer Resort at Chengde, Gugong: The Forbidden City, Mt. Huang-shan, Gui-lin, and Jiuzhaigou Falls. After visiting the photo gallery, go to **Focus on China** and visit the sections on the land, the history, the people, the structure of the state, the national economy, and the culture. Continue with information on the history and cooking techniques of Chinese food, and conclude with a little Chinese music. This site provides a great introduction to a fascinating country and culture.

Activity:

Build a miniature replica of the Great Wall by using sugar cubes as building blocks. Find a long surface and let the children go to work, using the pictures from the website as their guide. You can make either a temporary wall by stacking the cubes, or a permanent structure by adding glue in between layers of the wall.

Materials:

Sugar cubes
Glue

World Travel

Website:

World Surfari

Address:

http://www.supersurf.com/menu.htm

Surf the globe to learn a foreign language or explore the culture of a distant land. Go on a **Surfari** to Japan, Greenland, Italy, Kenya, or Jamaica. Kids can trace the country's history, visit the people, find out about the culture, or look up tasty ethnic recipes with a click of the mouse. Locate long-lost relatives at the **Fun from Afar** page. To learn the language of a particular country, type into a window the English word you want translated and, presto, the word is presented in Spanish, Italian, or Japanese.

Activity:

A child's parents, grandparents, or great-grandparents may have come from different parts of the world. Research each child's family history. You may want to send a basic questionare home for parents to answer. From what part of the world did their ancestors come? Allow each student to design and create a family crest that includes their cultural heritage. Create the crest out of anything—paint, colored pencils or crayons, or even a computer design program. Help them learn a little of their distant relative's language by trying out the language database at the website.

Materials:

Anything you want from which to create a family crest (paint, clay, plaster of paris)

The Internet started as a military experiment in the mid 1970's. The military wanted to design a network capable of sending packets of text-only information through computers. Eventually, a few networking specialists in the private sector enhanced the technology, from which evolved the ability to send multimedia documents as well as text. The result is the Internet we use today.

No one organization controls the Internet. However, there are several organizations and corporations that have great influence over the Internet. Regulation of the Internet will be an interesting issue of the 21st Century as governments and companies around the world attempt to exert their influence.

History and Government

Wonders of the Ancient World

Website:

The Seven Wonders of the Ancient World

Address:

http://pharos.bu.edu/Egypt/Wonders/

Travel back in time to discover the **Seven Wonders of the Ancient World**. The list dates back as far as 200 BC, but only one of the original seven remains today. Discover which one it is. One of the wonders was featured on ancient Roman and Greek coins, just as famous buildings are featured on coins and paper currency today. Learn the history and culture of an ancient civilization. The Statue of Zeus at Olympia comes from the same area in which the Olympic games originated. How could civilizations build such magnificent structures without machines? Follow the links to view **Wonders of the Modern World**.

Activity:

Cook up homemade modeling dough for the kids, so they can try replicating the Seven Wonders of the World as well as creating a few modern wonders of their own. Mix together 2 cups of flour, 1 cup of salt, 2 cups of water, 2 tablespoons of vegetable oil, ½ cup of cream of tartar, and a couple of drops of food coloring. Cook on medium heat for 3–5 minutes. Allow the dough to cool, knead it until smooth, and hand it to your kids for making their own wonders. The dough needs to be sealed tightly and stored in the refrigerator.

Materials:

2 cups flour	1 cup salt
2 cups water	2 Tbls. vegetable oil
½ cup cream of tartar	Food coloring

Conquer the Castles of Europe

Website:

Castles on the Web

Address:

http://www.castlesontheweb.com

Travel back in time and conquer the castles of Europe at this informative site. Take a virtual tour of over 70 castles and view pictures of many more. March over to the **Kid's Page** and enter **Ian's Land of Castles** to learn why castles were built in the first place and what castle life was like. Find out what castles were made of and how they were used as a defense against other people and wild animals. Kids can follow James the Jingling Jester across the web to learn about the Middle Ages, and if they can answer the *King's Challenge* they become a knight!

Activity:

Little lords and ladies can make their own fortresses with that most prized childhood possession, the empty appliance box. Adults can cut out a door and windows with a knife, then turn the box over to the kids. Encourage them to paint and decorate the castle inside and out. Pretend your class or family lives in it. Where do you get your water? What do you do for fun?

Materials:

Appliance boxes (call and ask an appliance store to save some for you)
Paint
Paint brushes

Dress–Up Disguises

Website:

CIA kid's Page

Address:

http://www.odci.gov/cia/ciakids/

Enter into the secret world of the Central Intelligence Agency, and explore the world of espionage as you try on several disguises. Choose from the traditional trench coat, hippie hair and sunglasses, or experiment with the not-so-popular moose ears and arrowheads. Flip through the **Geography** pages so your little globetrotter can learn all about the continents and international diversity. What country in North America is the largest? Is the temperature in Australia warmer in July or February? Trot on over to the **Canine** pages to meet Bo and his buddies, the dogs in CIA's Canine Corps. Bo has been with the CIA since he was a puppy. Watch a video on dog training, and print out a badge with a picture of your favorite guard dog. Fly with aerial photography pigeons as they show you pictures they have taken. Discover how an unknown spy named "355" changed history.

Activity:

Kids love to dress up and play pretend in a world of fantasy and make-believe. Use different disguises to make up a game of dress-up charades. Take turns dressing up and acting out different people, characters, and occupations. Play with your children, and see if you can guess who they are.

Materials:

      Clothes
      Hats
      Sunglasses and shoes

Flag Facts

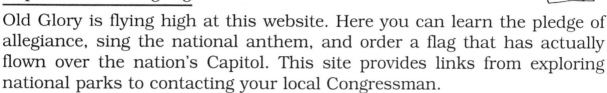

Website:

Flag of the United States of America

Address:

http://www.usflag.org

Old Glory is flying high at this website. Here you can learn the pledge of allegiance, sing the national anthem, and order a flag that has actually flown over the nation's Capitol. This site provides links from exploring national parks to contacting your local Congressman.

Website:

The Canadian Flag

Address:

http://canada.gc.ca/canadiana/flag_e.html

The Canadian flag has a rich and varied history. Come explore the story of the Canadian Flag—from the St. George's Cross of 1497 to the raising of the distinctly Canadian maple leaf flag in 1965.

Activity:

Create a personalized T-shirt to wear on the Fourth of July or Canada Day using student hand prints. Place a piece of cardboard in between the front and back of a pre-washed 100% cotton T-shirt, and lay it flat. Mix fabric paint separately with 50% fabric medium (found in craft stores). For an American flag, paint red and blue stripes on your children's hands using fabric paint. Place hands vertically on the front of the T-shirt and press firmly. For the stars, dip little fingers in white paint and firmly press in the upper left corner of the design. For a Canadian flag, paint a red rectangular background on the front of the T-shirt and let it dry. Create the maple leaf by dipping a child's hand in white fabric paint and gently pressing it in the center of the red rectangle. Cover the bottom of one foot with blue fabric paint and press on the shirt perpendicular to the flag design, to use as the flagpole. Your kids can parade the shirts on the Fourth of July or Canada Day.

Materials:

100% Cotton T-shirt	Red, white, and blue fabric paint
Cardboard	Fabric medium (found in craft stores)

Harriet Tubman

Website:

Harriet Tubman and the
Underground Railroad for Children

Address:

http://www2.1hric.org/pocantico/tubman/tubman.html

Learn about Harriet Tubman, the amazing American heroine who risked her life over and over again to free slaves. Mrs. Taverna's second grade class at Pocantico Hills School in Sleepy Hollow, New York, studied Harriet Tubman, then put together this wonderful website. Now, the rest of us can share in what they discovered. Read the timeline of Harriet Tubman's life (complete with pictures), take a quiz to test your child's knowledge of Harriet, and read character sketches about Ms. Tubman. There is a map of the Underground Railroad, crossword puzzles to complete, and ideas for classroom activities for teachers. This award-winning site is a wonderful example of what can be achieved by websites put together by young children.

> **Bonus site:** Harriet Tubman
>
> http://www.acusd.edu/~jdesmet/tubman.html
>
> Log on to this site for details on all aspects of Harriet's life.

Activity:

When the Underground Railroad was in existence, slaves hung quilts over the roofs of their homes for good luck. Make your own quilt with squares of fabric. Cut out squares of different fabrics and glue them together on a sheet of paper to make your own patchwork quilt. Hang it in your home or classroom—maybe it will bring you good luck!

Materials:

Fabric   Scissors   Glue

Historic Happenings

Website:
This Day in History

Address:
http://www.historychannel.com/thisday/today.html

Come find out what happened on this day in history or look up any other day of the year. Discover which famous person was born, what electrical gadget was invented, and what was happening politically or culturally. Click on the **Speeches** page to access the great speeches that influenced the course of history. Hear Neil Armstrong announce "That's one small step for man . . ." or Winston Churchill proclaim "We shall never surrender!" Go to the **Community** page to tour the online museum, and see the Great Empire of Rome, or Ellis Island. You can research automotive history, Civil War history, or Wall Street history. Try matching hieroglyphics in the *Pharaoh Game* or learn more historical facts with the *Fact of the Day* at the **Fun and Games** page.

Activity:
Mention the word "birthday" and every kid bubbles up with enthusiasm. Here is a chance to celebrate a child's birthday any day of the year. Go to the website, and read all about what happened on the day that each child was born. Which famous people share their birthday? Was something invented that day? Ask parents to provide baby pictures and stories of the day their child was born. Children love hearing the details of the day of their birth from their parents and sharing them in class. What did the doctor look like? What did Mom wear in the hospital? What did Dad do? These stories will make their birthday extra special.

Materials:
Baby pictures of students

Meet Thomas Edison

Website:

Time Line of Edison's Life

Address:

http://www.nps.gov/htdocs2/edis/old4/edison/timeline.htm

Inspire your children with the story of the life and times of Thomas Edison, the pioneer of electrical inventions who said, "Genius is 1% inspiration and 99% perspiration." There are nice photographs to accompany a detailed story of his life, as well as descriptions of the major events and inventions. Read about Edison's inventions, including the phonograph, the electric light system, and motion pictures, not to mention the 1,093 patents that Edison earned in his lifetime.

Activity:

Brainstorm with your children about an invention that they could make that would improve their lives. Is it a machine that cleans their room for them? An electric dog walker? How about an invention that automatically makes food they dislike disappear from their plates? Have them draw a detailed picture of what they would invent, then describe what it does and how it works. Talk about patents.

Materials:

Paper
Markers
Crayons

Tour the White House

Website:

The White House for Kids

Address:

http://www.whitehouse.gov

Open the doors to the White House, and come in for a visit at the **Kid's Page**. Discover fun facts—did you know that painters use 570 gallons of paint to cover the exterior of the White House? Inside you can visit the Red, Green, and Blue Rooms, as well as the Oval Office, State Dining Room, and East Room. Learn how each room was designed and decorated. Read about Fala, Franklin Roosevelt's cherished First Pet, and Macaroni the Pony, a gift from Lyndon Johnson to Caroline Kennedy. Write a letter to the President, Vice President, or First Lady. If you enter a return address, you should receive a letter back.

Activity:

Make pencil rubbing portraits of past presidents. Place a coin (quarter, dime, nickel, or penny) under a solid white piece of paper and gently rub from side to side with a pencil until the picture of the coin transfers onto the paper. You will find Washington on the quarter, Roosevelt on the dime, Jefferson on the nickel, and Lincoln on the penny. After making your mini-portrait gallery, discuss what made each president great (you can find this information at the website).

Materials:

> White paper (tracing paper works well)
> Coins
> Pencil

The Internet offers excellent web pages for just about every holiday or occasion, and can be used to supplement the celebration at home or in the classroom. The next time you host a birthday party, log on to http://www.historychannel.com/thisday/today.html (the **This Day in History** site), and give each child a printout of what happened on his or her birthday. Teachers can give this to their students as a birthday surprise. Seasonal classroom parties can be brought into the 21st century by logging on to appropriate websites and allowing the children to look through them as an alternative or complement to a craft.

Holidays

Halloween Haunt

Website:

Absolutely Halloween

Address:

http://www.geocities.com/Heartland/7134/Halloween/hall.htm

Grim goblins and fairy princesses come and join in the festive spirit of Halloween! Click on **A Scary Night** to read a Halloween story, and go over the **Rules for Halloween Safety**. For example, if you are going out to trick-or-treat, *never* go without an adult. Click on **Sounds of Fear** to hear spooky music theme songs from Casper the Friendly Ghost, The Adams Family, and many more. Your kids can make spooky Halloween decorations, complete coloring pages, and print invitation cards in the **Playground**. Create some wacky and wild critters with the **Crazy Monsters Game**. Your children can download everything they need to build their own model haunted house—or is that a haunted model house?

Activity:

Halloween is the one day of the year children and adults can be whomever or whatever they desire. Plan to make costumes for the entire family, and have your children help create the costumes. Be creative and ecologically responsible by using old stuff from around the house. Make a robot with old economy-size laundry detergent boxes. Cut out holes for the arms, and remove the top and bottom panels of the box to slide over your child's body. Connect two boxes together with tape and spray-paint silver. Make a jester's costume from colorful sweat clothes and a funny homemade hat. How about being a clown? Paint your face and throw on an old maternity outfit. The possibilities are limited only by your imagination.

Happy Chanukah

Website:

Torah Tots

Address:

http://www.torahtots.com/holidays/chanuka/chanuk.htm

Read the story of Chanukah, learn about the lighting of the Menorah, and how to play a game with dreidels. Play *Spin the Dreidel* online, as well as *Star Code, Replace the Latka,* and *Plopples.* There is also a Chanukah word find and coloring pages to print. You can listen to traditional holiday music, learn Jewish blessings, and make some Chanukah recipes. This site gives a nice explanation of the holiday as well as other Jewish holidays and traditions on the **Home** page.

Activity:

Make a menorah with empty paper towel or toilet paper rolls. Take nine cardboard rolls and leave one the original size. This one will go in the center. Separate the other rolls into four pairs and cut each pair down in 1-inch increments. Pair 1 will be cut down 1 inch, pair 2 will be cut down 2 inches, etc. Glue the tallest roll in the center of a piece of cardboard, then glue the remaining rolls, one on each side of the center roll, from tallest to smallest. Decorate the menorah with paint or markers, then glue pieces of yellow and orange tissue paper to the top to make the burning flames. Happy Chanukah!

Materials:

Paper towel and toilet paper rolls
Cardboard
Glue
Paint
Yellow and orange tissue paper

Santa Claus

Website:

Claus. com

Address:

http://www.claus.com

Go to the **North Pole Village,** and get acquainted with Santa and his elves at this perpetually popular holiday site. You can choose your own elf buddy, find out whether you have been deemed naughty or nice, visit the **Toy Workshop**, and follow Santa Claus' route on Christmas Eve. The site also has kid-in-mind holiday recipes, fun games, holiday karaoke, and instructions on how to e-mail Santa. A great site to explore on a cold December afternoon.

Activity:

Write that letter to Santa! Encourage your children to write as much as they can on their own, and help them with the rest. If the letter is put in the mail addressed to "Santa Claus, North Pole," the post office will do its best to see that every child gets a response from Santa. Remind your children about the importance of remembering everyone at Christmas, and suggest that they include a wish list for a child their age that might not otherwise receive anything. Decorate the letters to Santa with markers and stickers and make a color copy for their memory box. Then put it in an envelope and send it off. Merry Christmas!

Materials:

>   Pen and paper
>   Envelope and a stamp
>   Markers and stickers

Thanksgiving Tradition

Website:

Thanksgiving

Address:

http://www.night.net/thanksgiving/

The song "We Gather Together" is heard as you enter this Thanksgiving site. It reminds us that Thanksgiving Day is about more than good food—it is a day for reflection and expression of gratitude for the blessings in our lives. Your kids can learn about the first Thanksgiving with the Mayflower Pilgrims, as well as the First Thanksgiving Proclamation in 1676. Spend a day in the life of a Plymouth Plantation Pilgrim by taking a virtual tour of his hard but hopeful world. Go on a turkey hunt, sing some seasonal songs, or print out harvest pictures to color. You can issue special Thanksgiving certificates to say, "Thank you for . . . " at The **Thanksgiving Fun** page. The site provides great links to other Thanksgiving sites including that other Thanksgiving tradition, all-day football games.

Activity:

Start a Thanksgiving tradition that your family can enjoy for years to come. Begin keeping a family gratitude journal. Once a week, month, or year, get together as a family and talk about the things in your life for which you are grateful, individually and as a family. Write the list in a journal and date it. Every year at Thanksgiving, read the journal together aloud. Parents and children alike will enjoy the many happy memories.

Materials:

Writing journal

The science of how vast amounts of information can travel thousands of miles in a mere instant is a mystery to most of us. The answer to this mystery begins with the modem. Basically, the modem inside or outside your computer allows you to connect, via your phone line, to the Internet through an Internet Service Provider, or ISP. Once your ISP has established a connection to the Internet and you request a web address through your browser, the information is broken down into small groups called packets. Your computer receives and assembles the packets. If the website connection is delayed, it may be because an unreadable or damaged packet may have been sent. In that case, the damaged packet is returned while your computer waits for a readable replacement. Once the replacement arrives, the information is assembled and appears on your screen in the proper format. You are then ready to go!

Science

Airplane Encounter

Website:

Air Force Kid's Page

Address:

http://www.af.mil/aflinkjr/entrance.htm

Strap yourself in for some high-altitude adventures at this soaring site. Your child needs a pilot nickname for his or her personal ID badge when logging onto this site. Visit the **Airfield** to learn about the history of flight, the story of the famous Wright Brothers, and how airplanes fly using thrust and lift. Children can practice math skills with **Captain Zoom's Math Adventure**, an interactive story where kids solve problems using basic math to balance weight and ration fuel and supplies for successful missions. In the **Game Room**, kids can print out coloring pages, connect the dots, or write and publish their own headline news. Fly over to the **Airplane Factory** to find designs for paper airplanes, and discover the difference between a Broad Wing and Delta Wing. Soon, your kids will be able to help design airplanes of the future. Go to the **Post Office** page, and e-mail airborne postcards.

Activity:

Make paper airplanes in many shapes and sizes. Use different types and weights of paper (construction paper, paper bags, computer paper, small notepad paper). Which planes fly the farthest, the fastest, and the highest? What makes the airplanes stay in the air longer or fly further? Pick out your favorite planes and decorate them.

Materials:

Paper	Scissors
Tape	Crayons

All About Weather

Website:

Franklin's Forecast

Address:

http://sln.fi.edu/weather/index.html

This site allows children to become junior meteorologists and learn how weather forecasters make their predictions. Check today's weather, and investigate the latest weather technologies. This site gives you instructions on how to make your own weather station and notifies you of upcoming weather events. Read about the importance of satellites, the awesome power of lightning, and the way radar helps to predict the weather. There is even a section on careers in the field of weather prediction.

Activity:

Look up the weather in the newspaper to see how accurate the prediction for the day is. Based upon what you have learned at Franklin's Forecast, discuss how the meteorologist came to the conclusions that he or she did. Talk about what kind of weather you like and do not like, and why. What activities are possible in inclement weather? What do you like to do when it is cool and sunny? What kind of clothes do you wear when it is snowing outside?

Materials:

Newspaper

Beautiful Butterflies

Website:

Children's Butterfly Site

Address:

http://www.mesc.usgs.gov/butterfly/Butterly.html

The amazing, beautiful butterfly comes to life at this well-organized and interesting site. Print out coloring pages from each of the stages of a butterfly's life cycle, and view a gallery of photographs along with specific descriptions of each butterfly. There is also a page for frequently asked questions, such as "How can I catch a butterfly or moth?" or "What do butterflies eat?" If a student's question is not on the **FAQ** page, he or she can submit a question to the staff of the Midcontinent Ecological Science Center, the organization that sponsors this site. Resources for butterfly gardens and activities with butterflies can also be found here.

Activity:

Make a butterfly magnet. Glue two flat wooden ice cream spoons together into the shape of an X. After they dry, glue a clothespin in the center of the X. Paint your butterfly, or color with markers, then decorate with sequins or small buttons and beads. After the paint and glue have dried, turn the butterfly over and glue a magnet to the back. Let dry, then display on the refrigerator.

Materials:

      Two ice cream spoons
      Clothespin
      Paint or markers
      Sequins, buttons, and beads
      Magnet and glue

Environmental Escapade

Website:

The Adventures of Alex On-line

Address:

http://www.alextheape.com

Swing over to the **Mystic Jungle,** and hang around with Alex the Ape and his gang of environmental champions. The characters Nessa B. Wilderbeast, Tootsie, and Ranger Rollie show kids how to protect animals from the pollution created by scientist Dr. Ludlow and his zany sidekick, Lumpy. In **Dr. Ludlow's Mad Lab,** children can participate in wacky but safe experiments, learn recipes for "gross stuff," and perform practical jokes. Catch the **Jungle Tour Bus** for a safari around Mystic Island. Climb up to the **Kids Only Clubhouse** to go on a treasure hunt, make paper dolls, and learn all about the Gibbon ape.

Activity:

Create a fun chemistry lab for your spirited scientists! Individually fill and label small plastic cups with vinegar, salt, baking soda, watered-down dish detergent, and colored water (water mixed with food coloring) in red, blue, green, and yellow. Provide children with an empty plastic cup, a dropper, and craft sticks for stirring their concoctions. Boys and girls can experiment with chemical reaction as they mix different liquids. The children can watch with delight as their potions react. Your kids can practice color change, too!

Materials:

Small plastic cups	Vinegar
Baking soda	Dish detergent
Salt	Food coloring
Droppers	Craft sticks

Moon Walk

Website:

Kid's Rover
From Earth to the Moon

Address:

http://www.hbo.com/apollo/cmp/rover_main.html

No, the moon is not made of cheese, but someday you might be able to go there and pick a tomato or two. Learn about American astronaut Michael Foale, who grew the first seeds in space on the Space Station Mir. Soar over to the **Star** page to learn about constellations and how trillions of basketballs grouped together can equal the size of just one star. Dogs in space? You bet! Meet Laika, the galactic dog, in **Space Travel**. Build a planetarium, play *Count the Stars*, and plan your own constellation on the **Activities** page. Most children dream of space travel; in the flight simulator, they can pilot their own 3D spacecraft. Choose from a trip on the Apollo Spacecraft, a Saturn V launch, or a lunar module moon landing. Can you manage re-entry and splashdown? It takes a few minutes to download the free 3D player and set up the *Flight Simulator*, but it is well worth the wait.

Activity:

Create a moon landscape with a mud pie. You need a pie pan, dirt, water, rocks, and soap and water for cleanup. Mix dirt and water into the pan to make a gooey batter. Add rocks, broken twigs, or dried-up leaves. Smooth out the mixture and set to bake in the sun. Your mud pie, when it is dry, should resemble the terrain on the moon—barren, with no sign of life!

Materials:

Pie pan	Dirt
Water	Rocks, twigs, and leaves

116

Ms. Frizzle and Friends

Website:

The Magic School Bus®

Address:

http://place.scholastic.com/magicschoolbus/index.htm

If your family is not yet familiar with Ms. Frizzle, Liz, and the kids on the award-winning book series *The Magic School Bus*, by Joanna Cole, it is time you got acquainted. At this science-oriented site, your child can play *What Do You See?* and *Blows its Top*, two interactive games. Solve the *Riddle of the Week*, download coloring book pages, and join in the *Mystery Name Search*. Teachers will appreciate the **Teacher Feature**, which provides curriculum for science projects like *Close-Up on Rot* (recycling) and *Butterflies are Pretty Tricky* (what it is like to drink from a flower). You can also add works of art to the **Kids Art Gallery**, and find out if the traveling bus will be coming to a city near you.

Activity:

Conduct your own sink-or-float experiments using common classroom or household objects and a basin of water. Collect items from around the house such as a cork, a penny or other coin, a plastic straw, Styrofoam packaging, a small lid from a jar, dried beans, etc. Put a few inches of water in the basin and see which objects sink and which stay afloat. Discuss why this happens.

Materials:

Household or classroom objects to experiment with
Basin of water

Museum for the Mind

Website:

Fun Stuff Royal
Ontario Museum

Address:

http://www.rom.on.ca/eyouths/funstm.html

Your kids can spend the day walking in an archeologist's boots excavating artifacts at this virtual archeological site, and uncover cyber fossils, dinosaurs made out of chicken bones, and hieroglyphics! Learn about the strict guidelines archeologists must follow when digging for artifacts. The **Cuneiform to Computers** exhibit depicts the evolution of communication from prehistoric scribble to complex electronic documents zinging across the Pacific in seconds. Have your kids spell their names using the **Hieroglyphics Alphabet**. They can create their own mummy in the **Discovery Center**. Don't be afraid—the directions are for a pretend mini-mummy! Learn about evidence that suggests that birds descended from dinosaurs, and look at the dinosaur skeletons made out of chicken bones. Help animals find their proper habitat in *Biodiversity Bingo* on the **Web Activities** page.

Activity:

Be an archeologist for a day, and go for a dig in your backyard or local park. Get together shovels, buckets, a sifter, and an old toothbrush for gently removing the dirt from discovered artifacts. Proceed to an archeological site of your choice. Mark off the area to be excavated and get to work. Adults may want to bring along some treasure (gold painted rocks are fun) to bury.

Materials:

Small shovel
Sifter
Old toothbrush
Artifact/treasure
Bucket

Natural Disasters

Website:

FEMA for Kids

Address:

http://www.fema.gov/kids/

Introduce hurricanes, tsunami, and other natural disasters to your children at this informative and entertaining site. The older kids can tackle *Disaster Math*, where they calculate math problems with a weather twist. Younger children will enjoy the *Hurricane House*, where they can click on objects in the yard which may cause problems during a hurricane. There is a tsunami game, weather jokes, a maze, and a crossword puzzle.

Activity:

Read the book *Cloudy with a Chance of Meatballs*, a zany book about weather, by Judi Barrett. After you finish the book, have your kids write a story about a time when different things fall from the sky, such as snow, rain, or hail, or perhaps animals, flowers, or household objects. Have them illustrate their story.

Materials:

> *Cloudy with a Chance of Meatballs* by Judi Barrett
> Paper and pencil
> Crayons or markers

Our Nervous System

Website:

Neuroscience for Kids

Address:

http://weber.u.washington.edu/~chudler/neurok.html

How does the brain work? How big is it? Do people really use only 10% of their brains? Kids can find the answers to these questions and others at this nervous system workshop designed especially for kids. Boys and girls can measure their spinal cords and find out how much they weigh. **My Brain is Bigger than Your Brain** looks at the brain sizes of different animals. Compare the sizes of an elephant and a chimpanzee for an interesting surprise. Learn that most people are right-brained and right-handed, while only 10% of people are left-brained and left-handed. Find out what parts of the brain control sensations such as touch, pressure, or pain. Read and discuss the **10 Rules for Brain Health and Fitness**. Children can discover amazing animal senses, and learn why penguins have great vision under water. Try testing your senses at the **Games and Activities** page.

Activity:

Test your reflexes. Have your children sit straight up in the chair with their feet dangling down. Adults, gently tap 1 inch below their knee. What happens? Discuss why the leg jerks up. Reflexes are working all the time. Talk about how nerves affect you. What happens when you are startled? Count how many times you blink in a minute.

Recycling

Website:

Reuse, Recycle, and Save

Address:

http://www.eduplace.com/hac/reuse.html

Reuse, Recycle, and Save teaches children about caring for their environ-ment through projects and experiments. This site is part of the **Houghton Mifflin Home Activity Center**, which has an extensive list of fun family projects. **Are You a Water Waster?** teaches children about conserving water resources, while **Whasit?** and **Decoupage Wastebasket** encourages them to make something new from something old. Neat ideas to teach an important lesson.

Activity:

Make a sculpture out of recyclable materials. Save plastic food con-tainers, toilet paper and paper towel rolls, egg cartons, plastic fruit baskets, wrapping paper, and fabric scraps. Get out some glue and let your children create their own original sculpture. Add some stickers, markers, and paint and they will be busy for hours.

Materials:

> Glue
> Stickers
> Paint and markers
> Plastic food containers, egg cartons, fruit
> Baskets
> Cardboard rolls, wrapping paper and fabric scraps

Space Exploration

Website:

StarChild

Address:

http://starchild.gsfc.nasa.gov/docs/StarChild/StarChild.html

Blast off into outer space! Future astronomers can soar through the skies at this informative and fun-filled site. Travel into the **Solar System** to view and print pictures of the sun, moon, planets, comets, and asteroid belt. Jet over to **Space Stuff** to learn how Neil Armstrong, the first man on the moon, and Dr. Sally Ride, the first woman to orbit Earth, became astronauts. If you want to drop them a note, you can find their addresses here. Check out the *Black Hole* in the **Universe** section, then print out a 26-page workbook about the stars and far-off galaxies. *Level One* is for younger children and *Level Two* is for the big kids. This website is out of this world!

Activity:

Make your own hand-held telescope to gaze at the stars. Take an empty paper towel roll and tape a piece of construction paper over one end. Poke an eyehole through the paper. Cover the outside of the empty roll with foil, but leave one end open. On a clear evening go outside and wait for it to get dark. Use your telescope to find stars and constellations. Can your little astronomer find the moon, the Big Dipper and the Little Dipper? How far away are the stars? What are they made of?

Materials:

> Paper towel roll
> Construction paper
> Foil
> Glue
> Tape

The Human Body

Website:

The Yuckiest Site on the Internet

Address:

http://www.nj.com/yucky/

This site addresses the various systems of the human body and finds a fun and interesting way to educate children about anatomy and physiology. Everything you never wanted to know about the human body can be found on this graphic and descriptive site. Become informed about not only your vital organs, but also such things as dandruff, bad breath, snot and boogers, stinky pits, vomit, and enough other socially incorrect topics to last you a lifetime. Gross, disgusting, and nauseating—kids will love it.

Activity:

Outline your child's body while he lies down on a long piece of plain white paper. (You can also try this outside with sidewalk chalk.) When the outline is complete, have him draw in the heart, lungs, kidneys, and other vital organs with markers or crayons. Reference the website for the exact location of the organs. Talk about the functions of the various parts of the body.

Materials:

Roll of white paper
Pencil
Markers or crayons

Volcanoes

Website:

VolcanoWorld's Kids' Door

Address:

http://volcano.und.nodak.edu/vwdocs/kids/kids.html

Load up on volcano facts at **VolcanoWorld's Kids' Door**. Take a virtual field trip, make a volcano art project, go on an adventure with Rocky, the Volcano Creature. This NASA-sponsored site has great games, stories, quizzes, and contests, just for younger kids. Older kids can build a volcano online, unscramble volcano names, and connect the dots to make Mount Rainier. Investigate currently erupting volcanoes as well as volcanoes around the world, and view volcano video clips. A nice mix of education and entertainment.

Activity:

Make a vinegar volcano. Take a soda bottle and cover it with strips of papier-maché (mix 1½ cups of flour with 1 cup of water and 2 tablespoons of glue; dip strips of newspaper into solution and form a mountain around the bottle). Let it dry. Put two tablespoons of baking soda into the bottle, then add ¼ cup of liquid dish soap, two cups of vinegar, and one cup of water. Stand back at a safe distance, and watch your volcano erupt!

Materials:

Soda bottle	Glue
Flour	Water
Newspaper	Baking soda
Liquid dish soap	Vinegar

When you are participating in sports, you want to have fun, but you also want to strive to improve your performance by playing better. Often, better means faster. Exploring the Internet can be great fun, but sometimes you wish it were just a little faster. One of the ways to speed things up is by deleting your temporary Internet files. On AOL, you can do this by accessing your preferences (My AOL, then Preferences, then WWW) and clicking on Delete Temporary Internet Files. Find how to do this on at least one other system. If you have been accessing many different sites, using this function will help to free up memory storage space and should help things to move more quickly.

Sports

Shoot Some Hoops

Website:

The Official Site of the NBA

Address:

http://www.nba.com

Anything and everything you ever wanted to know about the National Basketball Association can be found here. Read about the draft, take the trivia challenge, vote for the best play of the playoffs and the team that you believe has improved the most. Get all the stats on your favorite players—number of points they have scored, highlights of their careers, and how many free throws they have made. There are photos of golden moments in NBA history as well as clips of the most recent playoffs. You can also request a free trial issue of *NBA Inside Stuff* magazine.

Activity:

Talk about your favorite players, what makes them exceptional athletes, which teams you like the best. Create a game where your children practice making baskets by dunking their dirty clothes into the laundry hamper. If you have a basketball hoop and it is a nice day, go outside and shoot some hoops. Who knows—you might be watching the next Michael Jordan or Cheryl Swoops!

Materials:

Basketball

Soccer Surfer

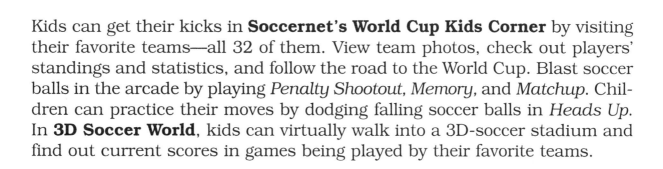

Website:

Soccernet World Cup

Address:

http://worldcup.soccernet.com/u/soccer/worldcup98/arcade/index.html

Kids can get their kicks in **Soccernet's World Cup Kids Corner** by visiting their favorite teams—all 32 of them. View team photos, check out players' standings and statistics, and follow the road to the World Cup. Blast soccer balls in the arcade by playing *Penalty Shootout, Memory,* and *Matchup.* Children can practice their moves by dodging falling soccer balls in *Heads Up.* In **3D Soccer World**, kids can virtually walk into a 3D-soccer stadium and find out current scores in games being played by their favorite teams.

Activity:

Master soccer skills with drills and games. First, teach your children which foot is right and which is left, where the heel and the ball of the foot are, and the difference between the inside and the outside of the foot. Play a game of *Hungry Wolf* using a soccer ball. One child tries to reach the other side of the field kicking a ball while the hungry wolf (an adult) tries to steal the ball. Practice rolling the ball around from the heel of the foot to the ball of the foot, first with the right foot, then with the left. Remember, boys and girls—little controlled kicks keep the ball within your reach!

Materials:

Soccer ball

The World of Sports

Website:

Sports Illustrated for Kids

Address:

http://www.sikids.com/index.html

There is a lot to do at this site. Here you can explore sports mysteries with Spooky Macgruder, get the latest on young athletes from the **Shorter Reporter**, and read the latest CNN updates on your sports heroes. Play great games like *Indy Car Racing, Mini Golf*, and *Snowboard Mt. Fuji.* Move on to **Buzz Beamer vs. the Green Monster** and take the *Buzz World Trivia Challenge.* Check out the **Funny Photo Studio** and write your own captions to go along with the sports shots. Your young sports fan will find facts and fun at this great sports site.

Activity:

Hold a mini-Olympics in your backyard or playgroud, basement or gym. Make up an obstacle course with old tires, hula hoops, a tunnel to crawl through, and sticks to jump across. Have a water balloon toss, and set up a bean bag throw or a basketball shoot. You could also have relay races with a potato balanced on a spoon, or a ping pong ball balanced on a paddle. Give ribbons to all participants.

Materials:

     Items for the obstacle course, e.g., old tires, sticks to jump over,
     Hula-hoops
     Water balloons
     Beanbags and large container to throw them in
     Potato and spoon or ping pong equipment
     Ribbons